Everyone's Guide
to (not) being an
Old Person

A fun handbook for anyone who knows someone who might be old, or doesn't want to get old themselves.

Robert Wingfield

Everyone's Guide to (not) being an Old Person

This work is sold subject to the condition that it shall not by way of trade or otherwise, be lent, resold, hired out, or otherwise circulated without the writer's prior consent, electronically or in any form of binding or cover other than the form in which it is published and without a similar condition including this condition being imposed on the subsequent purchaser. Replication or distribution of any part is strictly prohibited without the written permission of the copyright holder.

Copyright © 2015-2019 Robert Wingfield

www.cantbearsd.co.uk

All rights reserved.

ISBN 10: 1506006817

ISBN 13: 978-1506006819

Dedication

For m'dear mother, who is particularly good at not acting like an old person, and anyone else who has an older relative.

Contents

Introduction 1
What's Age All About? 2
Old Age and the Law 4
    The Law and Attacking People 6
    Paying bills 7
    Council Tax 8
On Routine 12
    Conclusion 16
On Stools (usually) 17
    Getting Things from High Places 18
    Defeating the Stool 20
    Addendum 22
On Bending and Grunting 23
On Religion 26
On Coats and other Clothing 31
    Sandals 33
    Sock Height vs. Age 34
Cars and Getting Around 35
    Parking 36
    Electric Cars? 37
    Hybrids 38
    Self-driving Cars 38
    What Car? 39
    The Hynishota Pointless 40
    The Hynishota Imagination 40
    The Hynishota Pig-Ugly 41
    The SUV or Hynishota Equivalent 41
    The Hat 42

The Mobility Scooter	43
Driving	45
Motorways	46
Touring	46
Local Traffic	48
On Money and Wills	**50**
Real Money	50
Options tried by Relatives	51
Credit cards	52
The Will	54
On Shopping	**56**
The Wheeled Shopping Basket	56
The Supermarket Trolley	58
Bargains	60
Shrink Wrap Packaging	61
Jumble Sales	62
Car-Boot Sales	63
The Post Office	64
On Doctors and Medicine	**66**
Chemists are great	67
Pills and more pills	68
On Shoes	**70**
Shoes in the Countryside	71
Old Person Slippers	73
A short guide to slippers	73
On Falling About	**76**
Stairs	77
Spectacles	78
Pavements	79
Slip-mats	80
Everyone is to Blame	**81**
The Blame Chart	83
Local Meetings	**84**
On Hair	**88**
Technical Things	**91**
Technology in General	91
The Internet	94
On Housing	**97**
Handymen and Local Suppliers	**100**

  Building work 101
  Appliances 102
  The Garden 103
  Which Garage? 103
On Caring for Older People 106
On The Weather 109
On General Chumminess 112
On Eating 114
  The Rules 117
On Death 118
  Cremation 120
  Standard Burial 120
  Standing Up 121
  A Vault 121
  Green Burial 122
  The Wake 123
  Pestilence 123
Things to do to Not be Old 124
Conclusion 130
Quiz to test if You really are Old 134
  Scoring 137
How Old Are You Really? 138

Acknowledgments

Gareth Jones for cover art and illustrations
http://gjonesart.com/
Dai Cooper and Bridget Parsonage for copy editing

Introduction

We all know someone older than we are. Some of us even have parents who might fit that description. There may also be folks out there you might describe as 'old people'.

Anyone can become an old person (OP), but what turns a perfectly level-headed human into an OP? We all get older, and at some point we might be worried about shifting into being an OP ourselves, or we may merely feel the need to mock someone who is displaying the symptoms.

This is a tongue-in-cheek manual for everyone; how to behave if you are an old person, how not to behave if you want to resist becoming an old person, or how to really have some fun gently mocking an old person.

Alas there is no secret to eternal youth revealed here (perhaps in the next study, due in 2090) but if you know what to look out for, you are in with a chance of a longer life; you will become to realise that getting old is a state of mind, not body, and if you really want to, can be avoided like a plague of boiled sweets (you know the ones).

What's Age All About?

Getting old; it's something we can all do if we are lucky, and practise a lot. With age comes wisdom, peace, and the kind of smugness that a Young Person (YP) can never hope to achieve.

It is perfectly possible to act young (or old) at any age, but if you behave younger you will certainly live longer (barring accidents or serious ailments) or at least be able to enjoy life well beyond the standard allocation of three score years and 90 pints of water.

Age, though, is a state of mind rather than an actual number of years. In the heady days of the 1950s, everyone over the age of 30 was old: they looked old, they dressed old, they acted old, and, according to the films of the time, most of them were in black and white. Since we discovered 'exercise', diets and face-creams not based on lead products, people can remain at almost any age they like. Old age happens when *you* decide to be old.

If you have bought this book for an OP, they probably won't be reading it, so you as a YP can amuse them by reading it out loud over a nice cup of Horlicks, and a lump of cake.

At the end of this expose is a quiz, with a view to finding out if you (or they) are old or not.

But what use is it all? None really, but a lot of fun, and if you giggle a bit during the reading, then it's all been worthwhile.

This tongue-in-cheek guide is written for everyone, not restricted to young or old people. It is not meant to be taken too seriously, so if you feel that you would like to be offended, please read no further. Instead you might consider a subscription to a popular newssheet, such as the *Daily Outrage* or the *Daily Inactivity*; you can be affronted regularly there, by all sorts of things, such as the fact that toilet rolls seem to have fewer sheets these days (and why is that?)

Your training as to how to be (or not to be!) an OP is covered in the following lessons:

Old Age and the Law

"The one great principle of English law is to make business for itself." **Charles Dickens**

It should be immediately noted that in the United Kingdom the 'law of the land' does not apply to old people unless they really want it to, in which case it is essential to follow it with dedication.

If you fall foul of 'The Law', the older you are, the more likely you will find a sympathetic judge. If you do get sent down, it will most certainly be an open prison where the only security measure is a high kerb around the perimeter; they know you can't lift your feet up high enough to escape, and even if you could, you would be picked up by the men with the guard tortoises long before you got to the shark-infested moat.

There are a number of different activities in which you can indulge for the purpose of provoking the people in blue (I don't mean home-helps, I was referring to our excellent and dedicated Police Force.)

Before we go further, I would recommend against trying the techniques here in other countries, unless they have a particularly kind disposition towards old folks. Possibly Denmark or Sweden would be places to try, but I would strongly advise against practising in Iran or some African countries, and definitely not in North Korea. Being old in these would probably bring too many other problems. It's not much fun being shot at; as an author with a large hat, I know all about this.

Having laid those ground rules, and assuming you aren't going to be persecuted for being old, apart from the usual suspects, (you know, the council, speed camera operators, parking wardens, and the people who hand out the food portions at the local carvery) we can proceed to general advice on how to behave as an OP in real-life situations.

The Law and Attacking People

As you know, young people these days are immoral and depraved. They hold hands and kiss each other in the street, even the girls, and they are not above going into pubs and drinking lager. They shout and sing, wear wellingtons at 'pop festivals' and throw litter about. Worse still, there seems to be an increasing number of folks who are not speaking your language. How can you complain about everything, if they don't understand what you are saying and just smile indulgently when you accost them? It is your job to police their behaviour, because nobody else seems to care.

For this you will need a large umbrella or walking-stick and a loud voice. If you see two people of the same sex holding hands, you wave your prop at them and exclaim that it is 'disgusting', pointing out the unfortunates to anyone who's attention you can attract. Better still, if you see people embracing, you can do all of the above, and then order them to stop, wielding your weapon in the air, or maybe poking them with it. Only do this in a busy environment though; there is an increasing trend for young people not to respect their elders, and they may strike you, causing not inconsiderable damage to your leathery skin.

If they do become violent, all is not lost; you can then roll around on the ground, shouting with agony, until the police come and arrest the felons, to put them into prison where they really belong, and can develop their drug habits properly. In certain circumstances you can suffer serious injuries and perhaps die, but you will expire happily, knowing that your assailant will be incarcerated for anything up to three months for murder, and learn what same-sex environments are all about.

Paying bills

Bills are always coming in through your letterbox, despite you having sealed it with duct tape. These should be paid immediately, and it is vital you go straight off to the bank to get cash or a cheque, to take in to the local office of the issuer. Paying by post or over the Internet is totally out of the question. The Internet is the Hammer of Satan!

Sometimes the local office can be in a different town. You can make a whole day of catching the bus and travelling, often in dreadful weather conditions, to a remote outpost where you have to wait in a queue with other old people, to pay it in. Here you can make a lot of new friends you will never see again, and complain about the waiting time, the weather and the reliability of the buses. "I hate being in queues," you can say, but have you realised that you *are* the queue? If you stayed at home or put a cheque in the post, or were able to use internet banking, it would not be necessary, but then you would miss out on the social interaction and the chance for a good moan.

Council Tax

How council tax is split among authorities, based on a Band D property			(2014/2015)
Authority	Amount	Percentage	Old Person
County council	£1,121.94	72.81%	0%
Police authority	£181.35	11.77%	0%
Rubbish Collection	£173.29	11.25%	0%
Fire authority	£64.26	4.17%	0%
Boiled sweets and cakes			100%
Total	£1,540.84	100%	100%

The council send you a bill every now and then for the services they provide. This is all very splendid, but why should you be paying for facilities you do not use? Examining them individually:

The Fire Service: How many times have you burned your house down this week? Well, there was that incident with the cigarette, where you went to sleep and set fire to your tablecloth, but that was only once... oh, and that time you forgot the gas was still alight on your stove, and put your oven gloves down on the burner, but apart from that...

The Police: How many times have you called the police out? Well, a lot really because of the neighbours, but how many times have they come out to see you? So why should you be paying for the police?

Rubbish collection: Because you do not bother eating, or like to store all your rubbish in the spare room, you have very little to throw away. What there is, you can sneak into the bin next door, when they put it out for emptying, the night before. This saves you having to lug your own down the path to the road. The Bin Persons used to collect it from where you hide it, but because of health and safety, they are not allowed to trespass on your property, in case they get bitten by your pet crocodile (who is only playing really) and collect it themselves.

You conclude that the Council are not really doing anything for you, so why pay the costs and have to stand in the queue at the Town Hall? You ignore the bill.

Subsequently you get lots of paperwork through the post, in varying shades of red. These can be safely ignored, including the summons asking you to go to court. How are you going to afford to travel that far in your present state of infirmity and poverty, you reason?

Eventually, some people turn up at the door to invite you to explain your actions. You perhaps see your local police for the first time. The best policy is not to let them in. "How do I know you're not conmen trying to cheat me out of my life savings?" you bluff. They show you their badges and the summons, but you can't see them because you've lost your glasses. You can however, use the opportunity to complain about the neighbours, and the dog mess on the pavement.

Ultimately, the authorities lose patience with you, break in, and take you to court. You get a nice ride in a police car and can chat to the officers on the way, telling them all about your health problems, and which of your neighbours has died this week.

In the courtroom, they read the charges, and you explain you are not paying, because you do not receive any benefits from the Council. They refuse to accept this as a defence, even though you have the moral high ground, and tell you that you have to pay the bill, plus a fine for not paying the bill. You act confused, pretending not to understand, and the nice policemen take you home again.

As soon as they leave, you can telephone the local newspaper and tell them you are being victimised. The reporter is almost instantly at your door, scenting a 'human interest' story to put beside the one with the complaints of the family of 14 who are having to pay bedroom tax on their 12 bedroom, taxpayer-funded mansion.

You still resist any bills or fines. After a period of time, the bailiffs turn up to take your prized possession away. You do not let them in, because it is not convenient, and tell them to return in an hour with a warrant. They have a warrant, they say, but you cannot read it because you have still not found your glasses. You agree that they can come back in an hour. During this respite, you call the newspaper and by the time the bailiffs return, there is the hack and a man with a camera in attendance.

Everything is recorded, including your wailing and the rending of what's left of your hair, and they film you pathetically hanging on to the coat of the man who is taking your television. There is a national outcry because, after all, did you not fight for your country, so that everyone today can be free? You probably did not, but that is of no consequence to the papers. It becomes a national incident, you gain your five minutes of celebrity and sell your life story to one of the glossy magazines at a fat profit. You can then pay the bills. Everyone is satisfied.

You might not, however, get the media coverage you crave, people dismissing you as a 'miserly old soak', but in this case, you refuse to allow anyone in your house until they actually break down the door and drag you off to an open prison somewhere in the country (see earlier).

Once in, you can stay there as long as you like, at the taxpayer's expense, being waiting on hand and foot, all meals provided etc. This is an acceptable alternative to becoming rich via your life story, and has the added benefit that you are not confined to an old folks home, where you are forced to watch your fellow inmates die off one by one, and can never find the remote for the television.

Final Thought: All this aside, if you own your house and have nice things inside, and a reasonable pension, then it is probably best to get your children to pay the Council Tax for you, because they don't want to see their poor old parent dragged into disrepute.

On Routine

"Habit and routine have an unbelievable power to waste and destroy." **Henri de Lubac**

"I like having a routine, because everything else… is so unpredictable." **Jordana Brewster**

One of the skills you really need in order to be an effective old person is the ability to impose a rigid routine upon yourself. Having the time mapped out is very important, so you cannot tell one week from the next. As you get older, the weeks, months and years literally fly by, and this is a great way to get through all that tedious extra time you have been blessed with, now that your children are fending for themselves, and not visiting because they have families of their own (unless they get you to babysit).

Here is a suggested order of tasks to get you through the week. Note that they must be as inflexible as possible so that you can have a good moan about people not coming to see you:

Monday:

Washing. You probably have a few clothes, soiled cloths, drug money, blood-stained murder weapons etc. that need to be laundered. Monday is the day you *have* to wash, whatever the weather. You might have allowed your offspring to provide you with a washing machine, but you cannot get on with that, so you do everything by hand; it's cleaner that way. This can take the full day, and has the added advantage that it makes your hands look like withered prunes. You could then dry your washing on the line, but too often in our blessed country the weather will not permit this, so you have airers loaded with dripping clothing scattered around your house. This not only allows the attire to get that nice musty smell you love, but fills the house with water-vapour, so that you can breathe better.

Tuesday:

Shopping. If you cannot get your offspring to do it all for you, you can roll your trolley down to the local shops and spend more money than you had planned, because local shops are never as cheap as the supermarkets. You know this, and complain bitterly about it, but it is important to support your local facilities.

Wednesday:

A day off. You can relax and sit in front of daytime TV if you like; there are always interesting antiques or house improvement shows on during the afternoon, for you to take seriously and then bore your friends and relations with.

Thursday:

Hairdresser, chiropodist, doctor, handyman etc. Thursday is a busy day. You are exhausted after this and have to go to bed early.

Friday:

Various activity groups around the area. There is always a charity or religious establishment that has a coffee morning, beetle drive, bingo or indoor skateboarding to keep you amused. You can spend your time there, shouting at people who can't hear you because they haven't put their hearing aids in, either.

Saturday:

Or Sunday, see below. A day of prayer groups, jumble sales, complaining, and tea and cakes.

Sunday morning:

(Or Saturday, or not at all, depending on your religion) Devotions. These are usually so exhausting that you need the rest of the day to recover. You are unable to see anyone afterwards, unless they have come from the church/mosque/temple/pub/football stadium etc. that you are devoted to.

Every afternoon:

Daytime television has a certain appeal. These days, the essential show 'How Clean is your Countryside Deal in the Attic' is always on, and if you miss an episode, you will have thrown the entire fabric of the universe into disarray. For this reason, you must never answer the telephone or entertain visitors at this time, or if you are forced to, by stealth or misfortune, you have to sound as grumpy as possible so that it never happens again.

Meals:

These have to be taken at precisely the same time each day. If you do not do this, you will instantly fade away and die of malnutrition. Five minutes either way is not too big a deal, but you will soon be feeling faint, if you allow the delay to extend any more than half an hour. If someone has the nerve to call you during that period, you must always continue eating, and talk through mouthfuls of food, chewing as loudly as possible in order to convey the message that you are not to be disturbed, in future.

Evening television/radio:

After dinner, the News must be assimilated in case you missed anything in the other 5 bulletins you've listened to that day. After making yourself miserable with the depressing broadcast, a radio programme, such as 'The Archers', can be enjoyed; if you nod off during it, you can always catch up with the omnibus edition. After this, there is usually a gloomy soap to watch, probably named after a neglected part of town, again during which you shall not be disturbed. If anyone recommends an interesting programme for you to watch later, you can politely decline, and explain that your eyes are tired.

Conclusion

So really, if you have anyone who cares about you, it is best to give them a detailed timetable of your activities during the week. They can then arrange their visits/calls to avoid disturbing your carefully planned schedules. Don't forget though to never write anything down for them. This has the advantage of you being able to tell them over and over again, what you are going to be doing, and fills time a conversation would otherwise occupy.

And why should you have an agenda? The main reason is so that all the weeks run together, and it is all leading to the end of the year, when you can say mystifyingly, "I just don't know where the time goes these days."

On Stools (usually)

"I love climbing because it feels so good when I stop..."
Karl Baba

Not the toilet kind of stool, and we are going to resist the temptation of 'daily movements' gags, but the rickety, usually three-legged style, that is particularly good at throwing you to the floor. Occasionally these can be substituted for dining chairs, particularly the type made of matchwood, and upholstered with springy seats.

Getting Things from High Places

It is a fallacy, if you are an Old Person, to say you can still look after yourself. You can potter around the house doing the imaginary daily chores: ironing, dusting, vacuuming, running a brothel, etc. which fill all your time, in comparative safety. There are always tall cupboards in your house though, or a collection of memorabilia stuffed on the top of a wardrobe.

It suddenly becomes a major objective to sort through some of this material at the precise time you are completely unsupervised. Hidden in a cupboard or under the stairs, you have treasured an antique stool. This device has been used for raising you to the necessary height for many years now, and is still serviceable, even if the ancient gum that held it together has long since biodegraded.

In order to climb up high, you must place this lethal piece of equipment slightly too far away from the target furniture, mainly because you cannot bend that far down to get it any closer. You will then be able to haul yourself up to the desired altitude. You know that the stool is rickety, so you hold on tightly while ascending.

You locate the target artefact, but it is a bit heavy for these rarely used arms, and both hands are necessary to extract it from the pile of other forgotten artefacts. As you recollect from primary school (quite clearly, although you can't remember what you did yesterday), you are now exhibiting one of the applications of the Law of Balance. You are standing on the stool, with both hands full, and on one leg because you need the other to step down. As you might expect, and realise as you are flying untidily towards the floor, the items will go in three separate directions, usually accompanied by painful crashing and splintering.

There are two possible outcomes:

1. You have done yourself a serious injury, in which case you can lie on the floor, attracting hypothermia and spiders, for an unspecified amount of time, before someone comes to find why you aren't accepting the free papers and plastic begging envelopes supplied by the charities. If you are still breathing, you are sent off to hospital where you can spend a pleasant afternoon on a stretcher in a corridor waiting to see a harassed doctor.

2. You survive, with no life-threatening injuries. In this instance, you must not mention it unless someone notices your bruises, when you are allowed to feel stupid for having put yourself in such a situation. You must vow to never do it again. The broken stool or chair is repaired using an impact adhesive bought from the local shop, and returned to its original storage, ready for a repeat of the performance next time there is need. This will eventually lead to the law of averages revisiting point 1, and you ending up in hospital, or worse.

Defeating the Stool

Once your caring family have realised that you have one of these evil devices, they will probably buy you a steadier piece of furniture to stand on. These can be in plastic or wood, and are very robust and stable. They are also not very expensive. The family may first ask you to think about buying one for yourself, but this contravenes the 'Rule of Money', where nothing is spent, except where something tried and trusted has eventually failed or been eaten by woodworm. You decline to invest but promise that you will never use said chair/stool/bucket/trapeze again, and that you will always ask a younger person to climb up for you in future. This can be either a direct lie, or conveniently forgotten by the next time something is needed.

Once they find you on the floor again, surrounded by fractured memorabilia, the YP will probably buy the new support for you, using money they have had to reallocate from their fag and drug habit (you suspect). Out of gratitude, you will promise to use it all the time, and they take away the three-legged murderer and hide it.

You eventually need to track the stool down, because you desperately want to look at your 100 yards swimming trophy. You have the usual problems. The very next day, your YP spots some new bruises. You try to be evasive, but crack under torture, and admit that you have again been mountaineering.

"Why did you not use this beautiful new sturdy thing we got you?" they ask.

"It's too heavy," you reply.

"Why did you not say that after I built it and showed you how to stand on it?"

"I did not want to hurt your feelings," you can reply,

or

"It got in the way, so I put it in the shed,"

or

"I've always used my stool. It's an antique. It took me ages to find it. Don't hide it again."

They disappear, muttering things that would make a Bulgarian Navvy blush, and return with a light foldup plastic step. They inform you that this is convenient, because it weighs less than a fashion model, and can be stacked sideways in one of your many spider refuges in the kitchen. They even show you how to open it. To begin, you must feign stupidity, but despite this, you eventually have to admit it really is simple, and get the hang of picking it up in the right place so that it unfolds properly. They leave you to practise, taking away the impression of a job well done, but a wise YP will have a nagging feeling at the back of their mind that this is not the end of the troubles.

The following week alas, they are proved right. The three-legged stool is back, and new bruises have appeared on you, to join the collection. The relatives will again show you how to work both new stools, and you are forced to promise you will never again search for the Three-Legged-Stool-of-Satan. While you are making the tea, they go outside to the shed, and saw the legs off the TLSoS, wrap the remains in newspaper and conceal it in the neighbour's bin. Apparently it has been proved by scientific research that this is the only secure way of keeping you out of hospital. You are furious; that stool has been in the family since you found it in a jumble-sale last year.

Addendum

Alternative solutions such as putting things down on a lower shelf are not really worth the bother. If you see an empty shelf, or surface of any kind, you must consider it a challenge to fill that space with other tat. It is there that the charity shop or stall, or the church bring-rubbish-and-buy-junk sale comes into its own, but that is another story.

On Bending and Grunting

"You can get far in North America with laconic grunts."
Ian Fleming

As an OP, it is vitally important to grunt at every available opportunity. This conveys the message to young people that you are suffering, and is intended to garner sympathy, and possibly a free lunch. It is suspected, though, that young people do not react to anything of this nature, except by telling you to, "Buck up, and get more exercise." In the worst case, they say, "What do you mean sitting about all day and hardly using your muscles, and then expecting us to be sympathetic?"

Do not be fazed by this. Old folks should practise grunts, and be prepared to use them as often as possible.

As a guide, here are a variety of grunts, and the occasions you might want to consider using them. The audio book will make more sense, but I'll try to summarise the sounds one might expect to hear.

1. **The sitting down grunt**: Exhale gently as you lower yourself into the chair. It would normally be a sigh, but by using the back of the throat, you can make it sound more effective. It can also be complimented with a slight bleat of pain, not enough to deafen the neighbours, but sufficient to attract the attention of any visitors you may have.

2. **The getting up grunt**: This is much more hard work. You have to roll forward in your armchair and use what remains of the muscles in your arms to push yourself off. You can accompany this with a louder grunt than before and also a slight whimper.

Caring children may offer to purchase you a seat driven by electric motors, so that you can get it to push you forward and upwards without all the effort, but it is important to decline this, as it is too easy to rewire; you are not ready for 230 Volts, and them getting their hands on your fortune just yet.

3. **The bending down grunt**: On attempting to pick things up from anything below waist height, bend at the middle (never the knees) and let out a simultaneous sigh and grunt. You can also augment this by complaining

that you can't bend down, because it makes you dizzy, and requesting that your young companion get the item for you.

4. **The getting into the car grunt**: Some kind people might like to take an OP out for a drive. Normally, this will involve a Hynishota Pointless, with the doors designed specifically for folks of anorexic disposition. Getting into one of these is a trial, but gives the opportunity for the issue of a special grunt: exasperation, pain and effort all in one.

Once inside there are supplementary grunts whilst finding the most uncomfortable position to sit in the seat and then fumbling for the seatbelt, which is behind you and you can't twist to see it. The YP might kindly hand it to you, and then you have the satisfaction of more groans and whines as you fail to find the slot to plug it in, and get it wedged between the seat and that strange bulge in the middle of the car, you know, the one that nobody can tell you about.

5. **The being helped moan**: If someone tries to assist you in standing up, getting out of a car, crossing the road, etc. they may try to take your arm, and guide you. If they apply any pressure on you at all, you can give the special cry, which would make a flock of seagulls weep. It is intended to make them feel ashamed of their very existence, and take up a religion where they can have weekly visits to plead for the absolution of their sins - see next chapter.

On Religion

"The problem with writing about religion is that you run the risk of offending sincerely religious people, and then they come after you with machetes." **Dave Barry**

Religion comes in many forms, but is basically anything you do with dedication. Yahoo defines it as "*A cause, principle, or activity pursued with zeal or conscientious devotion*", so you can take that to include football, knitting, antiques, cakes, human sacrifice, harlots etc. Your deity can take many forms, from the manager of your football team, through Derek Dickenson, Big Gloria, Darth Vader, and onwards to one of the more conventional leaders such as Allah, Lao-Tsu, Kim Jong-un or the Almighty. Whatever religion you follow, it is fine if not taken to extremes.

Religion is something that you as an OP do really well. There are concerns amongst the attendees of various churches, synagogues, mosques, temples, bordellos, etc. that, as the faithful pass on, they will not be replaced by the youngsters, who would rather be out working to pay for old folks' pensions, getting drunk, fighting, shouting, or just finding a nice other-half with whom to spend their days in bliss.

I can inform you that this is not the case. Some religions have a dedicated, sometimes fanatical attendance amongst the younger generation, and those that perhaps have less appeal for the excitement and machismo, still have a few younger people, who have seen whatever light is generated by those particular establishments. It may help you to know that as young people get older, or move to North Korea, they too will eventually join the congregations, as they attempt to discover some meaning in their lives, and need to atone for all the misdemeanours of youth (at which they are very good, these days, you may say).

Some young people will do this because they have been wrapped up in their day-to-day existence, and after a lifetime of their particular routine, are wondering if there is anything more to be discovered. Even in the hardiest, the prospect of impending death can jolt them towards religion, to see if it holds the answer. If nothing else, these establishments will almost certainly supply a good cup of tea and a cake at very reasonable prices.

If you want to have fun, try taking an outspoken child to one of these feasts. They will make observations about the older folks such as, "Grandma, why is that lady so fat?" or "What are all these zombies doing here?" or "What is that wizard over there wearing on his head?" Your comrades will then have to smile indulgently, and usually give the child a pound to go away. Note that this is an excellent way of boosting the small person's pocket money, if you happen to be a bit short yourself.

I could go in more detail into individual religions, but they all have common themes including:

Be nice to each other: always say 'hi' in the street, but don't slobber on people, or offer them boiled sweets.

Respect your dear old mum: only if she's still making scrummy pies and cakes, and doesn't insist in telling her cronies about all your distressing skin conditions.

Don't nick stuff off your neighbour: he will probably lend it to you, anyway, if you ask nicely. Most neighbours are good like this, if you offer them a beer in exchange. Those that aren't can be reported to the police at weekly intervals.

Treat other people as you want them to treat you: why not invite that vagrant back to your home for an evening of Mah Jong and ale. In return, he might ask you back to his cardboard box, for sardines and meth, where you can learn how fortunate you actually are... or be relieved of your valuables.

Always tell the truth: unless you are speaking to the taxman or street-beggar, or trying to get on an 18-30 holiday.

There is only one God: Actually, everyone thinks their own God is the One, but the truth is that he, she or it has loads of different email addresses, all redirecting to the same mailbox. If you happen to believe that there is no God at all, then that mailbox is probably stored somewhere in Google's Cloud, with a 'Do-not-reply' flag on it.

It's better to give than receive: this applies especially at Christmas, when you would rather smite the advertisers with a stout stick, than receive their sickly commercials for the best part of three months. It also relates if you happen to be a burglar, where breaking in and leaving stuff rather than taking it, will make you into a hero.

Do not harm anything living: except those awful houseflies or mosquitos—what use on Earth do they have then? This 'harm' thing extends to respecting the planet, not scattering litter about, and cleaning up after your dog.

Blessed are the pacemakers* (for they givest thou good heart and cheer) and allow you a full and active life, with that young person you met on the Net, and who is presently spending your considerable pension pot.

Love your enemies but don't lend them money or your hedge-trimmer. Forget transgressions, but never forget names.

Do not kill anyone: even if they do have their own opinions about something, or support Rangers. Killing people who do not agree with you is a waste of time. They might have a valid point for you to consider, or they might be talked round to your way of thinking, or they might be going to buy you a half of 'Stout'. They can't do that if they're leaking blood on to your quarry-tiles, now can they?

Wisdom is more precious than riches: the jury is out on this one. If you've got no money at all, then it's hard to be wise, unless that wisdom involves giving up fags and booze and drugs, which may be the fundamental reasons for your poverty.

And the best of all "**Honour the elderly**": they are so disrespectful, young people these days, aren't they?

* This was actually 'peacemakers', but if everyone behaved themselves, people who make peace would not be necessary. For the OP, perhaps pacemakers would be more use, especially if you have a dubious ticker.. or then again, you might just like motorsports (pace car).

On Coats and other Clothing

"I was raised in California, so this whole New York winter thing is completely new for me. I've already justified buying seven coats!" **Blake Lively**

By now, as an OP, you have accumulated a good selection of clothing, which has been fashionable during parts of all of the last 60 years. You don't want to throw anything away, or buy anything new (except from a charity shop) because they made things to last in those days, and the item will 'see you out'. The temptation of the many bags for clothing collections that are shoved through your letterbox is easily resisted, and these bags make great liners for your swing-bin, saving you money in replacements from the Pound Shop.

So you get dressed to go out, wearing several layers of items that have serviced you well for the last century… As an aside, some archaeologists swear by the rings caused, and theorise that if you cut an OP in half, you can see layers of clothing dating back to before most people were born. Some even argue that they can tell the age of an OP in this manner, but Society takes a dim view of sawing old folks in half (except in hospital) and it is almost never put into practice in this country.

Once you have listened to three or four weather forecasts for the day, you can then leave the house. It is important to add an extra layer of coats, just in case they got the temperatures wrong; after all, with these new measurements, how do you know whether you are hot or cold? It never happened with Mr Fahrenheit's values. You knew where you were, then. The climate has gone out of control since temperatures became Centigrade; yet another plan to confuse people, like when they changed understandable telephone numbers like Whitehall 1212 into a string of meaningless numerals, thrice!

Sandals

Now if you happen to be the outdoor male OP, and the weather is warm, then sandals and socks are the essential outfit. It is thought that you can also tell the age of a man to the nearest decade by observing the height to which the sock is pulled up the calf. Sandals cannot be worn without socks, because they are usually so badly fitting that they would cause callouses.

To begin with, the man experiments with short socks, perhaps stealing some unused 'pop socks' from the 1980s, but this quickly descends into tennis socks, which can be had by the bale from the local pound shop, and although they last only 10 minutes in ordinary shoes, can have quite a full life in sandals. The added benefit is that when they wear out, the damage and hole is instantly visible so that your significant other can bin them without telling you, before they get any worse.

As the man gets older, he pulls the socks up higher and higher, as the indents in his unused calf muscles support them. Once exceeding a certain height, ideally one should then go to football socks, but these are expensive, and imply some affiliation with the indicated tribe, which could be dangerous, should one run into rival supporters, and is to be avoided. Also if challenged wearing football socks, it is not wise to suggest that all football supporters are probably gay, because they like to watch men in short trousers running around, falling over, and kissing each other. If they were real men, they would watch women's rugby, you say, which *is* scary.

Everyone's Guide to (not) being an Old Person

Sock Height vs. Age

100 Getting Kinky

90 – Support Stockings

80 Still rambling

70 Now no shame

60 Starting to go

50 Style failure

Stunt Legs posed by actor

Cars and Getting Around

"In less enlightened times, the best way to impress women was to own a hot car. But women wised up and realized it was better to buy their own hot cars so they wouldn't have to ride around with jerks."
Scott Adams

C ars are essential for the OP. Once you get past a certain age, you realise that buying the idyllic cottage in the country was not such a great idea with the nearest shop 150 miles away. As you *are* an OP, you haven't mastered the idea of ordering your shopping over the Internet, and therefore have to visit the local shops at least once a day, to buy those essential items you forgot the day before.

The personal transport does have uses other than taking you to the shops. There are too many cars on the road at certain times, so if you are particularly perceptive, you can ensure you are always out at that time, along with them. It might take ages to beat your way along with the traffic but it has advantages:

- The engine has plenty of time to warm up so that you don't have to replace those expensive complicated parts too often.

- You can catch up on the omnibus of 'The Archers' on Radio 4.

- You never have to exceed 20 miles per hour. It is well known that all modern cars explode if going any faster than this.

- Sitting in a queue is a lot safer than out on the open road. It is like sitting in your front room, only eventually you will make it to the shops.

Once you get there though, you have to contend with Parking.

Parking

Parking is however easy. As soon as you exceed a certain weight, you can apply for a 'disabled' badge. This allows you to ease your car into town and abandon it in a space with that wheelchair/petrol-pump logo on it. This sign is meant to tantalise you because there is no way you can afford petrol on your pension. It is usually best to get someone else to drive you in and loan the badge to them for the duration.

Electric Cars?

What a great idea eh? Clean and silent and can be driven into big cities without paying pollution charges. There are a number of things to bear in mind:

- You can't magic energy from nowhere. It has to be created by something, nuclear power-station, coal burners or oil. If you are lucky, you will have sustainable energy sources like wind or tide, but these are not the mainstream just yet.
- You can't get energy for free. You have to pay for it in one way or another. One thing they won't tell you is how much your electricity bill goes up when you charge your machine from your house. I would guess it will scare you to death.
- Can the electricity supply cope? No. As was proved recently in the US, one of the grids overloading took down a quarter of the country. Where will you're your car be when you can't recharge it?
- Are you happy with a minimum range before recharging? On a frosty day with heater and everything running, your driving range before recharge will be a lot less than you have been told.
- Are you happy while waiting for your car to recharge? You might be able to go shopping and leave it at a charging point, but when electric cars become more common, you won't be able to get near it. People are selfish and won't bother moving their car when it is

recharged. You only have to queue at a filling station when the price of petrol is due to go up to see just how selfish and greedy some people can be.

Hybrids

These are a combination of petrol engine and electric generator, which charge the batteries while you are running on petrol, and can be used on electricity when in traffic jams or towns. The batteries also recharge when going downhill or braking. If you have to feel as though you are helping the planet, and don't mind the weight of the car, the reduced mileage, reduced storage space, or the risk of the batteries exploding when you crash, then feel free to go with one of these.

Self-driving Cars

Forget it. The idea of a self-driving car is a great one, but the designers and spin-doctors are not considering the people.

People do stupid things, like leaping in front of you from behind a skip. If you were in control, you would be ready for it, having picked up on the excess of psychic vibes from the moron who is going to attempt this feat, just to see how the car will react.

People do malicious things. They know your car will stop if they step out in front of you, so they do that, and an accomplice smashes your window and steals your wallet.

People do clever things. Self-driving cars rely on sensors and GPS (for the OP, GPS is a way that all the governments of the world can pinpoint your exact location to the nearest metre, using satellites armed with deadly lasers); in short, technology. Technology is clever, but can always be controlled by people who are more clever. They can put your brakes on for you, or steer you into a river, or switch your lights off when you need them most. In the event of a real cyber war (and World War Three will certainly take this form), the first things to go will be the satellites, and the technology in your car.

You don't need to worry, really. The overload on the electricity grid will cause a fatal shutdown long before you get your self-driving electric car any distance from your house.

What Car?

Having talked you out of self-driving death-traps, you should now be looking for a more conventional vehicle. If you are one of those lucky OPs who have had a good job and saved up a nice nest-egg without having it plundered by government, and/or big business, or the bloke fixing your roof, and you have decided to spend it on yourself (which you should, rather than saving it up to give to those relatives who never come to visit), then a new car is essential. You don't want a second-hand one because those are inherently unreliable, aren't they? Well if it was that reliable, why is the previous owner selling it?

There is only one choice for a new car if you are an OP; the Hynishota Range (the actual name changed for reasons of litigation, but you know of what I speak). These vehicles retain their value, are reliable, comfortable, simple to operate, and carry the status symbol that says, "I'm a sensible and careful driver, if a bit of a dickhead".

But which one to buy? Here is a selection for you.

The Hynishota Pointless

This machine is small, economical, and totally without external features. It might be a bit of a squeeze to get in, but you will be comforted by the legacy of years of Eastern manufacturing from the days they were called 'Skosun' or something. Your last car was a Hynishota Pointless, so your new one should be the same. The designers have done a splendid job making the car even more featureless than before, so you can fade into anonymity wherever you go, and nobody will be bothered to ridicule you... unless you go for the bright yellow paint-job.

The Hynishota Imagination

Just when you thought that the Pointless could not get any more boring, and you need something you can squeeze into, those fine designers at Hynishota came up with the most amazingly simple project possible. Presumably born on the back of a fag packet, the 'Imagination' has done its best to copy that format.

This beautiful piece has all the advantages of the Pointless, but you can actually get into it, without having to bend double. Drive one of these around town and you will not only get a comfortable ride, space for your shopping, and fuel economy, but also sympathy from kind people, and contempt from those of an artistic nature, with whom you wouldn't want to associate anyway.

The Hynishota Pig-Ugly

If you want something even bigger, because you are lucky enough to still have your significant other with you, then you should probably buy the Hynishota Pig-Ugly. It has taken the designers simply years to come up with something quite so hideous.

On the plus side though, it is again rugged, reliable and spacious, for you to get shopping, wheelchair, golf-clubs, Labrador and everything else loaded into. It is also bigger, and therefore you stand less chance of being crushed to death in that multi-car pileup in the High Street, and if you get snow more than three feet deep, you still have radio reception, so you won't miss the news bulletins and weather forecasts.

The SUV or Hynishota Equivalent

This is the ultimate vehicle for getting yourself around, with the added bonus that you get $9000 if you can sell it to a mod shop in 'Grand Theft Auto V' without scratching the paintwork.

If you live anywhere near a tree, then you will need it for wandering up and down farm tracks in search of hidden ancient monuments, and to get your farm eggs and meat at inflated prices from the bizarrely named 'Farmers' Markets'. It is also good for car-boot sales, where you can get rid of that massive collection of boots you have amassed over the years, and bring home a completely new collection of otherwise useless items. A word of warning though; it is important to have your halogen headlights professionally adjusted so that they cause maximum irritation to the car in front, even when you are driving on dipped beam.

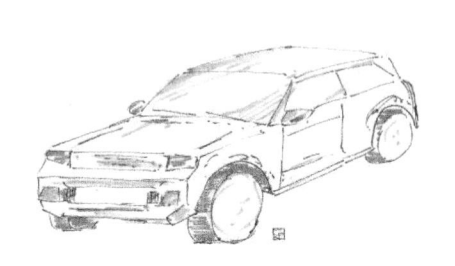

The Hat

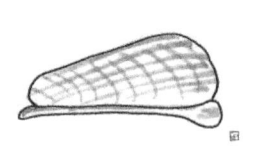

Finally, what would driving a car be without a hat? Originally, the 'Trilby' would be the annoying driver's headgear of choice. The hearts of brave men would sink if they got behind a driver in a Trilby, and plummet further if he was also smoking a pipe. Now, in these enlightened times, use of that particular style of hat is confined to eccentric authors and fictional private detectives, and the 'flat cap' has taken its place. These can be bought at most legacy outfitters, and will last you a lifetime of driving. As a bonus, they can be wrung apologetically when you meet the lady from 'the big house', and may also bring on the desire to speak with a North Country accent. They can even be used when not inside the vehicle, and will keep your head warm, even on the sunniest of days.

The Mobility Scooter

These are the most amazing things since someone decided that sliced bread was a good idea to use to illustrate amazing things. You can forget all about space travel, the jet engine, antibiotics and the mini-roundabout, sliced bread is the thing to be amazed about... and the mobility scooter.

Originally, there was a strange machine called the 'Invalid Carriage'. It was lethal, and probably a devious plot by the Government to reduce the number of people to whom they had to pay pensions. It is believed that you could kill the occupant simply by breathing too heavily on the paintwork, and fortunately has passed out of use since everyone that bought one has died horribly.

You will usually have to buy the mobility scooter yourself; it is not available through the Health Service who are busy spending the money on endless reorganisations, and if pushed can only authorise the loan of an embarrassing metal framework to trip you up.

If you have the money, (or can con your offspring) you can pick up a second hand mobility scooter, quite reasonably, and a lot cheaper than a Hynishota Embarrassment. They are best bought if you have never driven any wheeled vehicle before, so that you can cause the most amount of stress to those around you, while you career along, trying to remember which of the controls will stop you.

They are powered by electricity, and therefore are quiet enough to enable you to sneak up behind stout ladies and use your horn to make them jump out of their considerable skin. Being electric they (the scooters, not the large ladies) need charging up for quite a time before they will get you as far as the shops (again, the scooters, not the large ladies), which gives you the option of running out of power, before you make it home. You then have an excuse to call the YP who helped you buy it, and that way you see them more often, as they replace the battery. Use the phrase "I've broken down," because this sounds better than, "I forgot to charge it," and will elicit a more rapid and sympathetic response.

Once you have mastered the controls, you can then get people to ferry you in their Range-Rovers to car-boots, jumble sales and country walks. The latter are significant, because you will be able to get bogged down in so many different ways. Fortunately the wheels on your vehicle are interchangeable with those four wheel toys for the rich (or farmers) called quad-bikes. You can have your tyres replaced with an off-road variety, and that's where your interest in wildlife can be fully realised, as you churn the mud in search of exotic varieties of birds.

Being electric, and able to be driven on the pavement without a licence at speeds up to 4 miles per hour, these are excellent for getting around without any insurance.

Now that the tax disk has been discontinued, there is no way a policeman or traffic warden can penalise you for any misdemeanours. There is even one variety of scooter (Class 3) that will do up to 8 mph, but must be used on the roads themselves, and then with a suitable flashing beacon. Inexplicably, although you would not drive it on a motorway, dual carriageways *are* permitted, so if you are tired of life, or fancy a bit of excitement, then this is most exhilarating.

If you know a bit about electrics and motors, you will quickly realise that with a few modifications, the limiter can be disabled and it is perfectly possible to reach speeds of 40 mph, although you may need to hang on for dear life, and avoid any of the usual roadblocks set across the A14 to try to bring you to task. This is where you realise that air temperatures of less than 10 degrees Centigrade (that is something like minus 200 Fahrenheit for those of you still in the 19th Century, just after temperature had been invented) cause you to freeze solid, and contract hyperthermia, however many rugs you have included on your journey.

Problems aside though, the mobility scooter is something to really look forward to, and is one of the major perks of old age.

Driving

You may be sensible and not have a car, preferring to use the local taxi service for shopping trips, or public transport for longer journeys. After all you have a free bus pass; it would be a waste not to use it, and you can't actually find your feet anymore, let alone the road. However, if you do have your own transport, then there are a number of things to watch out for.

Motorways

If you can still see to get in to your car, and find the steering wheel, it is perfectly acceptable to drive your Hynishota Pointless at 30 miles an hour down the central lane of a motorway, hopefully in the same direction as the traffic. If stopped by the police, you act helpless and confused and make up a story about trying to avoid hitting a browsing deer. Most of the time, they will accept this, there being too much bother in the paperwork to proceed, and they have just witnessed a red Porsche buzzing past at 100, so let you off with a caution. Once you have set off again, you might have to move to the inside lane for a short while, and try to avoid the 'safety' cameras that are at 30 metre intervals along every motorway these days.

It is best to leave the motorway as soon as possible, because the B565678897 road which used to be the A10 will still be there, exactly as it was when you learned to drive, and you can potter along at your own speed annoying tractors, caravans and overladen lorries, that were desperate to be at the head of the traffic queue themselves.

Touring

If you are going any further than the shops, you can get out your tatty, but perfectly serviceable, road atlas from 1957, and plan a route. It will usually be a Sunday, because after a nice lunch at noon precisely, you feel that a Sunday afternoon drive is ideal for letting the food go down. You may even have some consideration for other drivers, thinking that they will all be down the pub or asleep, but more likely, you feel that Sunday is the only safe day to go out driving, because any other respectable road-users will be religious types, and therefore protected by 'divine providence'.

You decide upon the Cotswolds, because you used to go there on your bike when you were young, and they haven't changed that much over the years. It matters not that you lived in Cheltenham then, and now live in Bournemouth. The roads will be very pleasant today, because the sun is shining. Alas two-million other people have had the same idea, and most of them end up following you, getting more and more irritated. "There has probably been one of those pile-ups on the motorway," you think. "What a good idea we decided to go the back way." What you don't realise is that most of the other motorists are trying to get to the motorway in the first place, preferring to risk fiery death there, than sit behind you for another 50 miles.

You reach 'Long Burton in the Mire' eventually. There is still some daylight, so you get the canvas folding chairs out of the boot (or trunk, if you have the Hynishota Colonial), and place them next to the car. Mrs OP finds the flask of tea and the boiled egg sandwiches, and you sit there, gazing across the duck-pond, and watching out for traffic wardens who will be checking that you have paid £5 for the pleasure. As you understand it, you don't need a parking permit because you are not leaving the car, and technically you are 'waiting' if challenged. In extreme cases, and if they don't want to share your sandwiches, you may need to pack up and move along to the next picturesque village, where you might be able to find a pub that will make you a cup of tea and find you a nice piece of cake. The real OP never drinks coffee when out and about.

The journey home is slower. By now, all the people you held up on the way out have returned from hang-gliding, surfing, and drug-fuelled illegal raves, and you join the queue behind an overturned caravan, cursing and berating those sort of people for having the nerve to block the roads.

Many hours later, you reach home, grumpy, exhausted and sleepy because it's past your 8 o'clock bedtime. You vow to never to do that again, which is pointless because by this time next week you will have forgotten all about the experience, and be ready for another trip.

To try to get you out of your strop, Mrs OP tells you she really enjoyed the day. This does not help, and you retire for the night to nightmares of caravans and traffic wardens, and narrow twisty roads blocked by herds of caribou.

Local Traffic

On shorter distances, you can stop your car anywhere you like. There's Mrs Dingbat returning from her weekly visit to the chiropodist, so it is vital you pull up, and inquire about the state of her bunion, and update her on your own aches and pains, before offering her a lift home.

You have lived in the area for the past fifty years, so you know everyone over a certain age, and by the time you do eventually get home, you have used up most of your petrol (or electricity) delivering folks to their bungalows. The upside is that with more affable OPs, you are nearly always invited in, given a cup of tea and a slab of home-made cake. This saves money because you do not then have to feed yourself.

A word of warning; once the OP starts giving you cake

bought at the shops, they are most likely not long for this world, and you must make your excuses, in order to not witness their demise.

On Money and Wills

"The safest way to double your money is to fold it over and put it in your pocket." **Kin Hubbard**

Real Money

Cash is always a problem for old people. Either you have none at all, because you have been unfortunate and spent it having expensive holidays, drink, cigarettes, handy-men or call-girls, or you think you need to save it for a rainy day. Either way you begrudge every penny that leaves the purse. The exception to this is when an unsolicited workman arrives and gives you an inflated quote for something not really needed.

In this instance, money is no object, and the aforementioned labourer should be taken on a tour of the house, shown where the family jewels are hidden and provided *carte blanche* for the removal of cash.

Younger relatives will be left in shock at the rapidly diminishing family fortune, and may react with any of the following alternatives:

Options tried by Relatives

- They will attempt to gain control of your finances. This is usually doomed to failure. You would rather trust a handyman because he has a nice smile, than the person you have spent all their life bringing up. It says something for your confidence in parenting skills if you think you have trained your offspring to be that untrustworthy.

- They may attempt to get you to see reason. Again this is doomed to failure. You have spent all their life raising this young person, and telling them like it is. How would someone who was born this recently know anything about life and money and how to survive?

- In extreme cases, they might steal all your money and get you committed to a 'Retirement' home. This proves to you that all your fears from the first two points were founded, and you were correct not to give the dosh over freely. They do have a degree of immunity here, because it is rare that you will contact the police, much less press charges; you have a fear of the Constabulary and do not want to take up their time, when they should be catching hardened criminals such as speeding drivers, litter louts and people who have had a bit too much to drink, and just want to lie down in the street.

- Finally, they might try to persuade you to spend your money on something nice, for example a holiday in the sun, a new fridge, cooker, washing machine, car, entertainment centre, electric chair, etc. so that you can enjoy your twilight years. "Use the money," they say, "Make it work for you." This is the worst of the worst for you; you were brought up in times of austerity, and it is important that you retain as much cash as possible, in case it is needed for that 'emergency'. Or, you retain it to spend on a retirement home. Here, you can have exactly the same environment as a council-run establishment which you would be sent to, because you have none. Regarding any appliance in need of replacement, this is when you can use the trump-card phrase, "It'll see me out". The device they are talking about still works, just about, so why should you replace it, and have the bother of learning the controls all over again?

Credit cards

Credit cards are relatively new to the OP, and the idea of borrowing money to pay for groceries or other items is an alien concept. The fact that if you get the right card, you can get money-off vouchers, discounts and other perks, even donations to worthy charities at no extra cost to you, is unfathomable. "Cash is much easier," you argue. "You know where you are with cash, and it stops you spending too much."

The YP accepts that this is a valid argument, if you have no idea how to manage your money, but may point out that the security of the piece of plastic, not to mention the reduction in weight in your purse, more than compensates. You don't even need to remember your PIN, they will argue, with the contactless cards, and now that the providers have decided they are going to boost their security up to a point where scammers are finding it increasingly difficult to relieve you of your funds, it is a useful tool.

You still refuse, arguing that you have an extraordinary talent for sharing your security details with anyone who will listen. They suggest a special control which reduces the amount of money you can take on each trip out. They may also set up alerts so that every time cash is withdrawn, they will get a text to confirm. This way they can make sure you aren't ripped off, or at least if you are, only in small, traceable amounts. You have heard about 'Big Brother', and not from the television series, nod your head and make a silent promise to lose any card they force on you at every available opportunity.

What your YP doesn't realise is that if the card companies changed the description from 'Credit' to 'Advance Payment' Card, then you would be a lot happier, and would accept the benefits. You have always associated the word 'credit' with something that people did in bygone times when they ran out of gin money, and that is not you at all.

The Will

This is a piece of paper that suggests you may be of sound mind, a fact that your friends and relations vigorously challenge. You need one, so that your assets are fairly distributed amongst the people you specify, when you shuffle off your mortal.

A basic template can be downloaded for free from that Internet thing, but it is probably best to spend a load of money getting an identical one at your local solicitors. These learned personages will be only too happy to cross-question you on all the personal relationships with your family, so that only those who were your favourite children or grandchildren, even though they haven't been to see you since they were 10, get the proceeds.

If you don't do this, all those greedy b*****s who don't deserve it will find cash and Hynishotas a-plenty arriving at their doors. Do you want this to happen? If you aren't bothered, then <u>not</u> making a will is a really good way of irritating the family. Words like 'probate' and 'intestate' (not to be confused with 'inter-state', the roads in America, which are nothing to do with allocating your money, unless you use the tolls) and other such dodgy sounding legalese, are bandied about, and cause weeks of work before those slackers can get their hands on your effects.

There are then the months, if not years, of arguments amongst the family members and the falling-out of various factions over it. You can have an 'after-lifetime' of amusement watching the proceedings, and finding out if any of them actually liked you.

If you do decide to make a will, then you can make sure your estate goes to the right people and charities, and if your family has managed to ignore you all this time, it serves them right if they get 'squat', and have to do all the work to distribute it to the designated beneficiaries.

You should make sure you leave them your Hynishota though, in order to add embarrassment to insult.

On Shopping

"If men liked shopping, they'd call it research." **Cynthia Nelms**

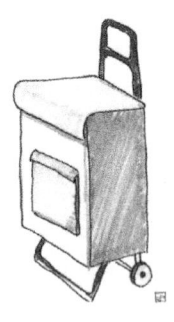

The Wheeled Shopping Basket

You have to leave home at precisely 08:45 each day, so that you are in town the moment the shops open. There are two benefits to this: the first being that you can do all your shopping nice and early, ahead of the rush, and be back home in time for the rest of the daily rituals. The second has an added advantage of being able to complain when you find that the bank doesn't open until 09:30 that day. Complaining is good; it gives you something to talk about to friends and relations, but problems should never be pointed out to the shops themselves, in case they do something about the shortcoming, and therefore remove your prime conversation material.

After a morning of bargains, spent knee-deep in other OPs with the same idea, you need some way of getting the loot home. Spoils though are normally quite heavy, having either been the jetsam of other households, or are the potatoes, tinned produce and cakes that you need to see you all the way through until tomorrow. This is where a wheeled basket is most useful. They are excellent for losing your purse at the bottom of—an added level of security—and also for towing weighty loads back to your home.

After the first few shops, you need to pay for something, and this is where you can unload all your shopping on to the counter, discussing each item as it appears. The system becomes self-regulating, in that when you repack your basket, you will almost invariably leave something behind. This can be repeated a number of times, before you return home exhausted. When you come to unpack, you realise you have left half your purchases behind, and then will have to retrace your steps to recover all the missing items, and enjoy the extra exercise.

This is where your faith in human nature is restored, because most of the shop assistants have seen what you have done, and will keep the items for you, pending your inevitable return.

As you visit each location, you can tell the kind people that you don't do this often, and will then be obliged to relate each of the preceding times when you have done the same thing. This will certainly brighten their day, and take their minds off the next seven hours they have to work until they can return home to housework, demanding children and ungrateful partners.

The Supermarket Trolley

RANDOM SHOPPING CARTS

LETTING PEOPLE KNOW THEY'RE IN A SHITTY NEIGHBOURHOOD SINCE ALWAYS.

www.funnywallphotos.com

Supermarkets are a comparatively new invention to you, and if you are brave, you can risk a visit. It is usually a younger relative who will try to introduce you to these, pretending that you can buy groceries more cheaply than at the market or the local shops. You visit to humour them, and find to your delight that there is a wheeled vehicle to assist you with your purchases, the supermarket trolley.

I won't bore you with endless complaints about the wheels and the way you can't push them all the way home without being arrested, or tipping your purchases into the gutter, so for the sake of this piece we will assume the device is sound and operational.

The trolley has limited use as a container for your shopping, because you are never going to be able to carry home the weight of your acquisitions anyway, so you can resign yourself to having a bit of fun, and pretending to be six years old again.

The supermarket will always have customers hurrying around, trying to fit in their shopping alongside their desperately busy day of work, children and rifle-shooting classes, and the trolley is excellent for interrupting their headlong trajectories. This will annoy them, but most people are too polite to do anything more than tut at you. Give yourself 10 points for a single tut or sigh, and 20 for anything more serious. If you suffer physical harm, give yourself 100 points and a trip to be murdered at the local hospital.

Here are some useful tactics, along with the extra scores you can award yourself for a successful result:

- Stop without warning: this is guaranteed to get some apologies, and perhaps even compensation as they ram their own trolleys into your back. At the very least you will slow them down and make them see the error of their ways, and at best you will make some new friends. **20 points.**

- Stop to chat: you can plan to meet your aging neighbour in Aisle 4, and you both wedge the place closed with your trolleys. Your conversation should be animated and loud, in order to prevent anyone from asking you to move. They will then try to push past, in which case you can berate them for being rude and inconsiderate. **30 points.**

- Stop to read the tins for additives: everything has these evil chemicals. You should pick up each item, fumble with your 'specs' and then read all the ingredients in detail. The activity will mean that you can completely hide that part of the shelf from any passers-by and slow the general flow. **20 points.**

- Look for the people loading the shelves. Always wedge your trolley in beside them to block the aisle. That way, the unfortunate employee will be berated, and have to apologise instead of you. **50 points**.
- Find someone loading a shelf, and ask them where the ice-cream sauces are stored. You can then leave your trolley next to theirs while you shuffle along behind the staff member. Points are awarded on return for the distance your trolley has been moved by other shoppers trying to get through. Along the same aisle **10 points per metre** (that is the same length as yards, only foreign). A different aisle **30 points**. Missing altogether **100 points** and a nice chat with the store manager, who will probably give you replacement shopping for free.

The target is to exceed 100 points per visit without being punched.

Bargains

It is essential to get bargains. You might not even need the items, but if they are a bargain, then they should not be ignored. You never know when they will come in handy.

If you see six for the price of five, then buy the six, even though you only need one. The surplus can go into stock, or even be foisted on to relatives and visitors to take away. Anything perishable can be hidden in the freezer and handed on in similar fashion. You will have a large stock of plastic carrier bags, so you can pack each item separately as you hand them over.

Look for bargains in the charity shops, on market stalls,

car-boot sales and from 'Honest John' down the road, but never in larger stores, as being trampled by other bargain hunters is not pleasant, and they are too self-obsessed to apologise. Remember though, that bargains are to be given away, not sold later by you at auction.

Shrink Wrap Packaging

If you buy pre-packaged food or bits of plastic for the kitchen, they are most likely sealed in the type of packaging that would keep the Crown Jewels safe.

Apart from being especially designed to choke dolphins, and fill up the seas, this sort of packaging is also specifically to stop the older person ever getting near anything that might harm them. Opening becomes increasingly difficult for the OP, as their unexercised fingers become more inflexible.

You start by searching for the tag that you know will remove the casing in a single pull. You locate it, and give a hearty tug. Your fingers slip. You struggle several times more, with the same result (an example of insanity; doing the same thing time and time again, and expecting different outcomes). Wiser now, and with sore thumbs, you use a pair of pliers, and succeed in tearing the corner off the package. Your newly purchased can-opener remains encased.

You try a pair of scissors, cut the package closer to the object and heave at the plastic again. No result. It seems that the packet is sealed all the way to the edge of the item. Again, you cut closer, and closer, and closer, and then right up against the device. At last the carton yields, and climbing over the pile of shredded plastic and cardboard, you can now extract your can-opener, and use it to get into that tin of sardines with the broken ring-pull.

You apply to the tin and squeeze hopefully. The can-opener bends and the handle falls off. If it had been unpackaged, you would have seen that defect right away. You abandon all hopes of an evening snack and the following day return to the shop, where you explain your problem.

The assistant looks at the devastation and nods sympathetically. "Sorry sir, we can't do anything for you because we have to return it in the original packaging."

History does not repeat your answer.

Warning: Opening yoghurt pots in the same way will result in excessive fallout, and ruin your best slippers.

Jumble Sales

These are normally for a charity, usually a decaying church or public building. You *have* to contribute, because it's all in a good cause, so you look around at tables of junk that nobody else wants, and spend the money on something you can't use, and will never need. The nice thing about this is that if the relatives won't take it to clutter up their own houses, then you can donate it as an item for the next jumble sale, preferably for a different good cause. There is the off chance that you might find something worth hundreds of pounds like people do on those afternoon TV greed fests, but how would you go about selling it, and what would you spend the proceeds on anyway? Money is less significant when you get older. If you have enough, then you don't need any more, you are told.

Experts have postulated that if you simply made a cash donation to the cause, you would have more effect and less bother, but that is not entering into the spirit of things, is it?

Car-Boot Sales

The car-boot sale is the new 'flea-market' as if you haven't enough fleas already. Everyone has items they don't need or use, or can't find a fence to take them off their hands, so they load up their van and visit a local field to palm them off on Eastern European immigrants. If you play your cards right, you can actually find things you don't need, for yourself, at one of these gatherings.

Choose a warm day, because forcing your way up and down a line of flimsy, decorating tables in a storm is not much fun, unless it happens to be in Wales, when those are normal conditions; I suspect they do not have outdoor boot sales in Scotland. With the right meteorological conditions, however, it is marvellous exercise. You can meander up and down the rows of tat, haggling with the desperate stallholders to reduce their 20p price-tag to 10p, and muttering under your breath that nobody seems to speak English any more.

The pleasure aside, I would strongly recommend against buying anything. If you do, it means you will have to drag it home, or for larger items, pay the stallholder to deliver. The latter course gives the excitement of a no-show, and a worry that you have wasted your money. However, when they do turn up with your decorated musical commode, you may be able to show them all your treasures for valuation, and perhaps they will offer you a fiver for the Faberge Egg your granddad left as an investment.

As you are planning to see all the stalls on the field, you might as well take your dog for the exercise. You may even be able to get away with not clearing up the mess, if nobody comments on where you empty your pooch. Either way, you can bore your pet to extremes, and even annoy people, when the mutt sniffs rear ends (if it can reach, or ankles if not), or stops suddenly to be fussed over by the numerous small children, who apparently have never seen a dog before. This is an antidote to those annoying other customers, with brats who are continuously whittling about buying that second-hand machine-gun for sale on one of the stalls; it splits families up and leaves parents rushing round madly searching for missing offspring, all to your amusement.

Finally, if you really fancy a challenge, take a small child along in a buggy. The child will usually insist on walking, and helping themselves to items off nearby stalls, but when you least expect, will start bawling, and have to be imprisoned in the pushchair, bribed with some piece of tat they have taken a shine to. The uneven fields then become almost impassable as you hit rut after rut. Hot, tired and annoyed, you eventually drag the ensemble back to your Hynishota Pig-Ugly, to drive home grumpily.

And that is what car-boot sales are all about.

The Post Office

Where would a trip to the shops be without the post office? These wonderful establishments are being closed down in all the villages that used to rely on them, mainly because the goods can't be sold at better prices than in the supermarkets, and people don't send letters anymore... except for you, and Mrs Goggins isn't going to be able to relay on your occasional visits to keep the place open. However, if you do have one, then pension day is the time to do all of your shopping.

You could quite easily get it paid into a bank account, but you don't trust these places. Look at all the problems they have had recently. Every week it seems that a system falls over, and people, who are unprepared enough not to have built any contingency into their financial arrangements, take to the streets in their outrage. It is far easier to be outraged, than to actually do something to protect yourself from these eventualities.

That aside, you queue up with all your aging chums, noting that the queue doesn't seem to get any shorter, despite the number of funerals you've been to recently, and eventually get a wad of cash that you can hide under your mattress, or spend immediately in the betting shop.

While you are there, of course, you can buy stamps and send out all the packages of tat that your relatives will put straight back in a charity shop, and this holds up the queue even more. Rural post offices are remarkably good at never having enough staff to cover at times they know will be busy: pension day, lunchtime, first thing, last thing etc. They are still run by individuals, who adhere to a strict routine, exactly like yourself, and these routines inevitable clash.

Of course, the main post offices are run more efficiently, but you never go there, because being herded like a line of sheep waiting for the delousing dip is demeaning, stressful, and they never put in any chairs for you to rest on, do they?

On Doctors and Medicine

"The desire to take medicine is perhaps the greatest feature which distinguishes man from animals."
William Osler

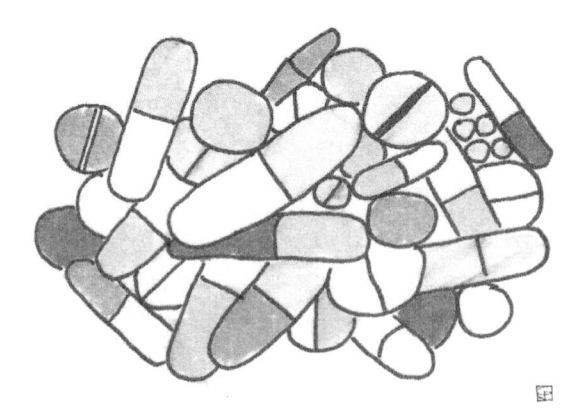

A wise old man once told me, "Keep clear of Doctors and Vicars and you'll live forever." Sadly he forgot to mention 'untrained Labradors', and on one occasion, he was tripped up by the said animal and hit his head. The doctors captured him, and kept him in hospital until they got the chance to murder him, for being too healthy at his age. This was many years ago, and the medical profession can now be relied upon not to give you any fatal diseases, unless you are unfortunate to go into hospital, or travel on the disease exchange system that is the urban underground railway, or know someone who has been anywhere near some parts of East Africa.

So, you have a twinge in your knee because you haven't used it for thirty years or so, and you pop along to see the doctor, after a wait of six weeks, for an appointment. He seems like a nice young man, if a bit preoccupied with 'patient throughput' as decreed by the Health Service. He listens politely to all your moans about aches and pains, but stops you when you get on to the weather and the state of the post office. At precisely 8 minutes into the consultation, he taps on his keyboard. A printer whirrs out a sheet of paper, which he hands over, avoids shaking hands with you, and ushers you out of the room, with instructions to take it down to the chemist.

Chemists are great

The shops are usually warm and cosy, smell slightly of disinfectant, and always have a few chairs for people to sit on while waiting for prescriptions. You can also stand in a queue with all the other sick folks, sharing their conversation, ailments and germs, until you get to the counter, and talk to a very attractive young lady who looks sixteen years old, about various private health problems you might be entertaining. If you are slightly deaf, you can shout, so that everyone in the shop can share your complications as well.

Eventually, you manage to hand over the prescription, or 'scrip' as it is known in more modern parlance, and the child shakes her head. "I'm sorry, we'll have to order that in for you," she says, "We don't carry it in stock."

You look at the mass of different coloured boxes on the

shelf behind her, and wonder what it is you have actually contracted that cannot be treated by any of those. You look worried.

"It's okay," she says, seeing your concern, "We will have it in by eleven tomorrow morning."

"Oh dear," you think, "That means I'll have to be in town again at that time, and tragically disrupt my routine."

"See you then," says the baby, and smiles brightly, dismissing you. "Next please."

When you do eventually get your 'scrip', you start taking the pills from the packet. Soon you've forgotten how many you have had, and a week later the box is empty, your knee still aches, you now feel sick all day. You book another appointment with the doctor, who, six weeks later, has turned into a lady.

"What happened to Doctor Gallipot?" you ask.

"He was a locum," replies the lady. "As am I. We are on placement before leaving for America where we can get paid a living wage. What can I do for you today?"

You note her nametag. "Well, Doctor Sangoma," you begin, "I've got this pain..."

Pills and more pills

After a repeat of the previous consultation to the nearest second, another visit to the chemist results in some more of the pills you were first prescribed, and an extra box, to take away the feeling of sickness caused by the first medication. These cause your heart to race, so six weeks later you get pills to slow it down. Now you feel faint and are given a new set by another doctor you have never seen before.

The process repeats, you seeing a different physician each time, and by the end of a few years you have to buy one of those useful pill dispensers, so that you can keep track of the mass of chemicals entering your body. Now you can take all the medication at the time you should have been doing over the last decade. Shortly afterwards, you find yourself lying on the floor with your head spinning, thinking that the marks on the ceiling are an invasion force of giant space artichokes, coming to steal your silver. It may be at this time you are lucky enough to have a YP to take you back to the doctor and have every single prescription cancelled to replace the lot with better diet and more exercise.

The moral of the story is detailed at the beginning of this section. Steer clear of doctors and the clergy, and **Avoid the Wild Labrador**.

Ailments are great though. Once you get over a certain age, each ache and twinge can be highlighted in graphic detail, and you can swap stories with your peers. The author's suggestion would be that you make an index of your contacts, versus complaints, and tick each box as the ailment is mentioned. Hey, you might even discover a trend, and expose the local authorities trying to murder you all, to save on pension payments. At least, you can have hours of amusement, and an excuse for carrying a clipboard everywhere.

On Shoes

"If the shoe fits, it's probably too expensive." **Adrienne Gusoff**

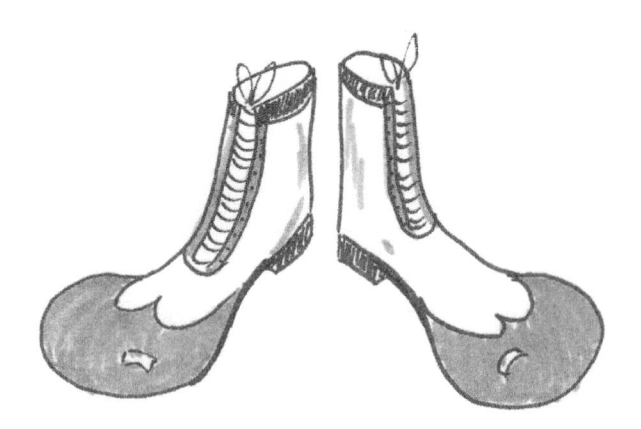

With age comes a change in the size and shape of the feet. Where you used to wear a size six, perhaps you now need a seven, to allow for the swelling brought on by the bucket of pills the doctor has given you for moaning about something else.

There are many different types of footwear on the market (or in the shops, or on-line), but if you can get what look like a comfortable pair of slip-ons from a charity shop then you will be in Seventh Heaven. These have the added benefit of not supporting your feet or ankles, and are particularly good at tripping you up and hurling you to the ground at every occasion.

Once you have these devices, which were either a bargain, or 'all in a good cause', you can wander aimlessly around town in them until a piece of uneven pavement pitches you to earth. The ambulance service are particularly good at picking up and comforting old people, so the accident rarely results in a visit to hospital. If you are an old lady, you may enjoy being manhandled by the sturdy paramedics, or firemen, if you've had a really complicated tumble, and can invite them home for tea and cake afterwards.

Shoes in the Countryside

For a different adventure, you can always ask a YP to accompany you on a walk into the countryside. Being a dutiful offspring, they will oblige, and you both find yourselves out in the wild world of farmers, nettles, dogging sites, gypsy encampments, and fresh air. With the outdoors, you will find the obstacles of uneven ground, mud, exposed roots and sharp bushes. Your YP will first attempt to steer you round these, but eventually you must insist on stepping in the right puddle.

This is where those special shoes from the charity shop come in. For a normal person, a sturdy boot or wellington would suffice to protect the feet, but you disappear into the sludge and require your YP to assist in the extraction. The shoe is nowhere to be seen after this, so you ask your YP to retrieve it from the mire, whilst supporting you, as you balance on one leg. They may grumble but you insist, and eventually the lost footgear is retrieved. After tipping out the mud, stones and tadpoles, you can return it to a foot.

You now have the opportunity for a long period of moaning and grunting, where every bump in the path or errant shrub is the fault of your YP. By the time you get back to the transport, their nerves will be frayed, and they will moan about the state of the carpets in the car for weeks afterwards.

There will be an awkward silence on the way home, but once there, you can tell them how much you enjoyed it and that you would like to do it again sometime. If they shudder and make some excuse about having to see your solicitor or doctor, apply that special OP expression you use to make them feel selfish and contrite, and they will finally agree to repeat the performance the following week.

Your YP may ask why you do not get some boots, or at least shoes that support better. You have to tell them that your ankles are swollen, and hurt when applying a boot. They may suggest that perhaps if a larger size was bought, it could be padded with socks. This is to be scornfully dismissed. "I have always been a size nine," you say, as if that were the answer to war and world poverty in a nutshell.

In the meantime, the original shoes are washed and they dry even more out of shape than ever. These are produced for the next adventure. If asked why you are still using such deformed footwear, you can firmly tell them: "These are my walking shoes."

Old Person Slippers

These deserve a section all to themselves. Slippers were originally used to avoid the cost of carpets, and the associated collection of bugs that makes its home within them. On bare floors, one could put these on one's feet and everywhere one went, it felt like walking on carpet.

The slipper was perfectly fine in its natural habitat of the Native American tepee, to protect against rattlesnakes and sharp sticks, or the Turkish harem, where the floor is of marble slabs for ease of scrubbing after parties, but these strange creatures have wheedled their way into the OP's home, and do their best to thin out the population at the earliest opportunity.

Those illustrated here are new versions, but you as an OP must keep them for as long as possible. Owing to the lack of stress the footgear gets, they are likely to last a long, long time. As the relics get older, they become more likely to trip you during the daily shuffle between cooker, television and fridge, and of course, when balancing on rickety three-legged stools.

A short guide to slippers

Type 1 slipper - the waste of money:

A nice snug fit to start with, and tends to keep the feet warm, but the problem is that after one or two insertions, the heel gets trodden down, and your foot swells, making it impossible to wear.

Type 2 slipper - the cosy toes:

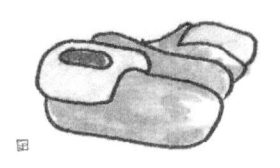

These are ideal to keep the feet warm on those cold evenings, and no matter what level of dilapidation can be kept for an infinite time, until they 'see you out'. You can also leave them in your Will to your next of kin, who by then will be long-in-the-tooth themselves. The smell from feet you are unable to reach to wash, ensures that there is no insect infestation in these items.

Type 3 Slipper - the Shuffle off your Mortal:

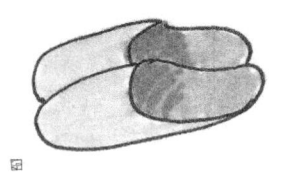

The most lethal type of slipper. They are easy to get into, which makes them attractive, as there is no bending required. In order to walk in these, you have to push your feet forward or you leave them on the floor and your toes get cold. You have to walk with the kind of shuffle that Egyptian mummies do in the films, and terrify small children who are needing the toilet. These slippers are particularly good at disengaging on stairs, leaving you tottering, and wishing you'd replaced the stair-carpet within the last century.

Type 4 Slipper - I yearn for the Great Plains:

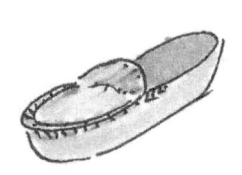

At least your feet would be warm on the savannah. These creations are usually made of stitched leather and will set rock-hard after a day of wear. This means that if your feet haven't moulded them into a comfortable shape by then, they alternately freeze your toes, and disconnect completely at inconvenient moments. You are safer on the stairs, because they have already flown off by themselves, the moment you raise one foot in the air. Not to be recommended unless you are hunting buffalo.

Type 5 Slipper - I can't bend or afford home help and actually can see the state of my tiles:

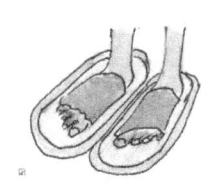

The only use these have is keeping the floor clean. If you have a carpet, they are difficult to move in, and therefore an ideal present for you, because it saves someone else having to do the floors. When the slippers get dirty, they can be popped in with the washing, and come up as good as new. This is one example of using unusual appliances for tasks - see 'Alternative uses for knitting needles and Sellotape' in the next volume.

On Falling About

"Our greatest glory is not in never falling, but in rising every time we fall." **Confucius**

By now you will have realised that with all the other hazards discussed, falling is what you as an OP do best. Based on previous lessons, we can summarise some causes for this:

Stairs

If you still live in a house, and haven't yet been incarcerated in a single-story building, then the likelihood is that the stairs within will be dark and steep. If they are carpeted, then it will be threadbare, loose, and may even be held in place with stair-rods. For those unfamiliar with Victorian engineering, the stair-rod was a cunning way of holding a carpet in place before glue was invented. The idea was that the material could be threaded under, in order to give the maximum chance of it shifting, as people walked downstairs. This is great for you, because the sudden upheaval is essential to launch you into space, where you may just have time to ponder as to whether the launch is due to slippers, carpet, the Three Legged Stool of Satan, or a simple assassination attempt by the offspring. Armour and a crash-helmet is recommended if you live in a real house, and have to go upstairs.

Normally you would expect to end in a crumpled heap in the hallway to amuse the postman, but as you can see in the illustration, if a small solid table is placed at the bottom, you can crack your skull open on that, or even shatter the glass of the vase and impale yourself on the shards.

Spectacles

Once one gets old, it is vital to compress what you used to call your glasses, goggles, bins, eyewear, contact lenses, monocles etc. into the word 'Spectacles'. If you are a particularly wacky OP, you can abbreviate this to 'Specs', or 'What the f* did I do with those things?'

These are especially designed to give you, the wearer, the best vision of whatever it was you told your optician you couldn't see. They are totally useless at showing you what you actually need in order to stay upright. Yes, you now have a good view of 'Ice Road Truckers', but try going up or down stairs in them and you are in big trouble. The distance between steps seems a lot less than it was before, so that you are always putting your weight on the foot that is in mid-air, and then scooting that little bit on your back or bottom. If you have a carer, they might notice this damage and call the police, who will go and arrest your children, the man next door or that nice chap delivering the commode—never the bailiffs, because they have a warrant!

The trick is to form a close relationship with an estate

agent or traffic warden and invite them around for tea; pain is turned into something useful, as they are marched off under suspicion that they have been abusing you (more than usual that is of course).

This 'depth of field' as techies like to call it also applies to objects on the floor, which seem at a different distance from your grasping hand. The kettle, the barbed wire and the crocodile you keep in the bath, can all cause you a serious injury.

Pavements

If you must walk to the shops, coffee morning, bring and buy sale, witch-trial etc., then you will probably use the pavement. I recommend this, in preference to the road, because, although drivers are supposed to give way to pedestrians, there is a fine line between crossing a road and 'jay-walking', which can be discussed at length with the driver of the white van, who has just swerved to avoid you.

Pavements, by definition are 'paved'. If they were of tarmac, they would be called something else; perhaps, 'macments', 'we were just round the corner and had some material spare'-ments, 'surface of the moon-ments' or some such. Paving slabs are relatively easy to lay, and look nice until the builder's lorry decides to park on them, or the earthworms and ants get a-tunnelling. After this, they (the paving slabs, not the ants) adopt degrees of unevenness depending on the substrate.

This all becomes an excellent tripping-ground for the OP, blinded by the wrong sort of glasses, and groggy because of the blow from the table at the bottom of the stairs and the cocktail of pills from the doctor. Often one of the utility companies will make sure of toppling an OP, by fitting raised ironworks, or digging up the pavement immediately after it has been laid, and replacing it with soft Tarmac, concrete, or cheese. They are also very good at blocking the entire pavement with their plastic barriers, and forcing the OP to cross the road into the snarling traffic.

Finally to make triply sure, irresponsible dog owners will empty their hounds right in the middle of the path, adding to the landscape of chip-papers, lager-cans, cigarette-butts, discarded syringes and broken glass, so often associated with some parts of town.

There is no way an OP is going to be able to get from one end of town to the other, without finding themselves face-down in something unpleasant, so the best option is to get a mobility scooter—discussed previously.

Slip-mats

Back in the days when carpets were rare and wore out before you could replace them, the OP (when they were a YP) would save the patches that were still serviceable, by cutting them into conveniently sized rectangles. These can either be stored in the attic, as habitat for spiders and wasps, or scattered around on polished floors to propel the OP across the room, whenever they stand on it. One could argue that the latter improves balance, or that it stands the OP in good stead for a visit to an ice-rink, but it usually is only good for keeping the ambulance people in work.

Other methods of toppling the OP include shoes, dogs, bear-traps, three-legged stools, and ambush by highwaymen.

Everyone is to Blame

"The man who can smile when things go wrong has thought of someone else he can blame it on." **Robert Bloch**

There are a lot of reasons for an OP to complain; missing items, the state of the world, young people, the Health Service, the buses, the traffic, the price of coal, noise, dogs, drugs, alcohol, the mastodon digging up your carrots etc. You might save time by considering becoming Scottish, where you can blame everything on the English, and not bother with the individual problems. If you don't, people might say that you are a natural moaner, and never satisfied with what you have.

One way of justifying this is to become a drug addict. In this instance it is *never* your fault. The 'Social' should be doing more, that guy should have never forced you to take that first hit, the chemist should keep your Meth for you, despite you forgetting to fill in the prescription, or turn up at the right time. Yes, you can give up the habit, but it is the fault of everyone else for not helping you.

There are problems. How are you going to chase around town at night, looking for dealers, in your condition? On the other hand, you have probably been given so many different potions by the doctor, that you could run a nice little industry from your bungalow, with the right marketing strategy, to supplement your meagre pension.

Blaming and complaining is something that you, as an OP, can make into a fine, art form. There is always something that needs to be corrected. To help, perhaps you can get the 'Daily Whine' delivered every morning. This noble rag details everything wrong with society, without ever trying to do anything about it, themselves. You now have a double footing for complaints, the misdemeanour itself, and the astonishment that the authorities aren't doing anything about it. This is what the rag is intending. If you have so much information about all the things wrong with the world, you might think that your voice will not be heard, and therefore restrict your complaints to anyone who will listen, as long as they are not in authority; you don't want to be seen as a miserable OP now do you?

Rather than going into a complete catalogue of all the things you can complain about, I would suggest you make a list, and award points when you find yourself focusing on a particular subject. See below for some examples, but you can add to the record as you go:

The Blame Chart

Subject	Can you do anything about it?	Points awarded
The Weather	No	5
Prices	No	5
The Government	No	10
The State of the Roads	No	5
Shop opening times	No	5
Traffic	No	5
Crime	No	10
Cats (or Ducks)	No	5
The Police	No	10
Young People	No	5
Neighbours	No	10
Broadband	No idea	100
Anti-social behaviour	Stop doing it	20
Tax	Spend your savings	20%
The Mastodon	Not without being stood on	20

Local Meetings

"I refuse to join any club that would have me as a member." **Groucho Marx**

Local meetings can take all sorts of forms, but the best plan is to avoid anything frequented by old people. Women's Meetings, Knitting Circles, Beetle Drives, Rotary Clubs, The Lions and Lionesses, the Conservative Party, Rambling Groups, Local Town Planners, Yoga etc. If you find yourself looking at a membership of people all the same age or older than you, then you are in the wrong place. These people will tell you about their own ailments, and cheer you up with tales of all ex members, who have passed on, and by the end of each meeting, you will find yourself depressed and believing that you are close to death yourself.

The best way to avoid this is not to pay any subscription up front, and refuse to be drawn by empty promises, such as they are hiring a coach for a day to go to the beach at Clacton, or are planning a lunch in a café in Sandringham.

If you are a man on his own, and really feel like the company of fellow humans, there are many ways to meet. The local public house may be a way of starting. Take a cute puppy or marmoset. Perhaps people won't talk to you to start with, except the landlady, who will call you 'my love'. This is not to be taken literally—you may have problems if you attempt to force your tongue down her throat—but is simply something to make you feel more at home, and is standard training along with the cellar-keepers qualifications that they need to run a pub effectively.

You will usually find a cosy corner to sit in and stare alternatively into your pint, or the fire for a long while, or until someone comes and offers you a cheap DVD. You won't make many friends this way.

If you really want someone to speak to you, then perch at the bar on one of those tall stools (not three-legged, you note). This can have two results, both breaking the ice. With luck, you will find someone on the stool next to you, and they will normally be talking about beer or football. You can then chip in and agree with everything they say, being careful not to call them a paedophile. This makes you very popular, and eventually they will offer to buy you a pint. It is good policy to reciprocate, so think very carefully before accepting it, taking note of the frequency of recall of the landlady, and the actual drink being ordered. Eventually you will have a group of new friends, who will always be there for you and ready to accompany on any binge. Given time you will even become part of the group, invited to accompany them on tours, usually breweries or pubs, but occasionally pubs and breweries, to break the monotony.

If, however, you are sitting on a large somebody else's stool, things can get ugly, especially if you decline to move elsewhere, so it is my advice that you apologise and vacate immediately. If you offer to buy the stool owner a pint, then you will straightaway make a new friend, with the added advantage that you will be well supported should a skirmish break out with the next stranger.

If all else fails and nobody will speak to you in the pub, then choose a time when there are only a few people in, and announce, "I've just won something in the Lottery; a drink for everyone (my love)." You will soon have lots of friends as the word gets round.

For a lady on her own wishing to meet new people, and you are not on the game, the pub is off limits, and you should consider the 'guided tour'. These can take any form, and as long as the walking is described as 'moderate', there will be no 'old' people to blight your life; you will meet like-minded folks, still in charge of their bodily functions.

Excursions can include full guided holidays (see my 'One Man in a Bus series' for examples of what to expect), tours of stately homes, nature reserves, castles, and best of all, ghost tours. This wonderful way of seeing a place at night (other than from the back of a Black-Maria) takes you into places you never knew about, and tells you tales of shock and horror. It matters not whether these are true, but at each juncture, you can grab the arm of the potential partner you have targeted, and pretend to be terrified. If the person is worth bothering with, they will comfort you for the rest of the tour and you can exchange telephone numbers and stalk them until they agree to go with you on other adventures. Be warned, this technique does not work with men stalking women, where it is called 'harassment', and will be dredged up thirty years later, when you are rich or famous enough for anyone to think you are worth suing.

On Hair

"I recorded my hair this morning; tonight I'm watching the highlights." **Jay London**

I f you are a man, hairdressing is easy. You simply go to the barbers with the most attractive Lithuanian ladies, and ask them to do the business. Sometimes they will cut your hair too, and in this instance whatever you have left on your head is reduced to a collection of wispy bits of grey on the floor, and the removal (at current rates) of £10 from your hard-earned betting money. This price does not vary, and can be found at most normal barbers, which is why the legs of the hairdresser become the deciding factor.

If you are a lady however, hairdressing is a completely different art. A lot of OPs are carrying too much weight. This is because of a number of contributing factors, such as lack of exercise, eating too many cakes, puddings or bags of chips, or being on the wrong pills, and at the change of life, or rarely, a 'medical condition'[1]. When you get to this stage, go into the cheapest hairdressers you can find and say, "Give me the 'fat lady' haircut please. I know you could make me look elegant like Joan Collins, but I do love Jo Brand, so that will do nicely."

What follows is the trainee's approximation of what Jo Brand would look like if she had a really bad haircut, and the removal of anything upwards from £15 from your handbag. You always pay cash as a matter of principle—credit cards are the signature of the devil—and book an appointment for the following week. This is useful because you can get them to wash your hair as well, which saves you the bother of lifting your arms, ever again.

If you ask nicely, they will dye your hair jet black, which with the change in colour of your skin makes you look like a Gothic tea-lady and frightens the children from the local school, so that they won't walk past your house anymore, and now have to be collected by their parents in Range-Rovers. There are other colours you can have, and hairdressers are specially trained to tell you that they like whatever you have chosen, without throwing

---

[1] This is what doctors call 'pigging out uncontrollably' when you are too scary for them to tell you the truth.

up on your floral print. To find an honest one you have to go a long way, and when they tell you that the style you are choosing does not suit your face, you have the option of ignoring them, because what do young people these days know anyway?

If you do listen, and the stylist is honest with you, you can actually come away with something that possibly makes you look younger into the bargain. When your offspring come round to visit, you might even get a compliment, and that could possibly encourage you to lose a bit of weight, or wear something more flattering next time.

Technical Things

"Any sufficiently advanced technology is indistinguishable from magic." **Arthur C. Clarke**

Technology in General

Technology is the word that young people use to describe new devices, such as iPhones, Tablets, Wifi, Bluetooth, the Internet, Engine Control Units, X-Box, remote controls and DVD players.

As an OP, if you feel particularly bold, you may make an attempt to purchase one of these inventions. You will find that the man in the shop will be only too happy to go through the operation with you, before he sells you one of the older models, which you have taken a fancy to because it reminds you of the commode that Grandma used to have. You have no idea how to use it, but think your YPs will be impressed when you show it to them.

The best policy with technology, though, is to avoid it. If you make an attempt to use any remote control box, you will find it has buttons which have been specified by a 12-year-old murderer, pretending to be a designer, and not tested on any humans. These buttons are each the size of a pin-head, and are in a bewildering pattern that defies all logic; the 'Delete all Recordings' button will be right next to the 'Play', the 'Mute' will be next to the 'Switch to the Porn Channel', and the 'On' switch will also operate the toaster and the games console next door. This is not good.

There is technology everywhere (I know, I've seen it!). You may have heard of the 'Internet of Things', which is a sneaky plan by the authorities to watch everything you are doing in the minutest detail. For example, your fridge will be able to tell you when you are running out of something, or that something is going past its expiry date. This will save you having to open the door at all, and conserve the associated energy. You could even leave it alone completely, and not bother putting anything in, just to spite the spies, although you might find the police breaking your door down, thinking that you have died.

Then there is your heating. You can now get a box, which will control that to the exact temperature you need. You can even switch it on remotely. This is handy when you are on holiday in Ibiza, and want to waste energy from a distance. While you are there, it will monitor room temperature precisely, so that even if you feel cold, you will know you are not, because your YP can check it on their phone.

Your car can now feed information back to your insurer via implanted technology, monitoring how slowly you drive, when and where you drive and if you are breaking any speed limits. The better you drive, the lower your premiums, they say. How soon before the traffic trolls get into that database and start sending you fines remotely, without ever having the pleasure of ridiculing your picture from some sneaky camera?

George Orwell talked about this sort of thing in his book, '1984', but people still do not believe it is happening. Try switching on the location app on your fondle-slab and let everyone watch exactly where you are. It won't be long before that becomes a permanent feature, everyone knows where you are, and the only way to turn it off will be via the use of a large hammer.

As an OP then, you must be very suspicious of this automation and pretend to be stupid and confused, in order not to have to use it. The YPs don't realise that is your plan, and will start saying they will put you in a home, unless they can hide some tracking device in your favourite slippers. The best way round this is to employ counter-technology; installing a jamming device in the form of a radio from the 1940s, or rewiring the internet connection to a mains plug.

If you really want to stay a young person, then embrace all this technology. Read the manuals, and practise when nobody is watching. When younger people come round to try out your Playstation 4, you can impress them by being better than they are at the games—it beats sitting the afternoon out with 'Greedy Bastards Antique Surprise' and can improve your mind and reflexes into the bargain. In a single sentence, to get into the Information Age, repeat after me "Technology is great. I need my house full of it."

The Internet

The Internet is really useful if you are housebound. By simply logging in, and connecting to one of the grocery sites, you can get the local supermarket to deliver everything you need directly to your door, at a time you specify. However, if you are a real OP, all this sorcery is totally unfathomable, and the confusion can be used as an excuse to get people running around, doing all your chores.

Another excuse not to use the Internet, can be the quality of the produce you will have delivered. Supermarkets get specialist pickers to choose the best of the products for you, but can you trust them? How do you know that when your bananas turn up, they are not over-ripe or bruised? What you've forgotten is that if this is the case, you can indulge in your favourite sport of complaining. Got a problem with your groceries, who are you going to call? The store manager is the obvious choice, and they are paid to be polite, whatever your problem, and are always keen to improve the quality of their service. However, this might actually resolve a perceived problem, so do not talk to them; your neighbours and friends are the best targets for that. You can bad-mouth your local supplier, without actually getting anything sorted out, and that is always the best policy.

There are many other uses for the Internet. If you are particularly astute, you can employ it to pester relatives who have moved long distances to get away from you. There used to be a free tool called 'Skype' which allowed you to actually see your distant kindred on the monitor screen, so that you can be pleased how old and haggard they are becoming, whilst telling them about which ailments belong to which neighbour. I say 'used to be', because it has been bought by Microsoft (2014), and will probably find its way into the next version of Windows, meaning that you will have to buy the next version of Windows at a seriously inflated price in order to use it. This also means that the lump of ancient computer offloaded on you by your grandson when he upgraded, although it used to work fine for Internet and Skype, will have to be replaced, leaving you with a bill and more clutter.

If you can get along with the Internet though, it is ideal for buying all those essential items you have seen advertised on the shopping channels at prices less than advertised. If you place your orders progressively, you can arrange to have objects turning up at your door every day. These are increasingly being delivered by couriers, who don't mind coming in for a chat and a nice piece of cake to break up their busy round. If you pay by credit-card, you can get all the goods before the bills come in, and if your balance becomes scary, can always pay it off with another card, or pretend to be dead so they write off the losses.

Finally, if you can't see the keyboard or screen, there are now excellent software packages which will read it out for you, and you can respond using voice recognition, which will relieve any loneliness you might try to develop as you try to get to grip with the interesting variations on the language that these packages produce.

On Housing

"Instead of getting married again, I'm going to find a woman I don't like and give her a house". **Lewis Grizzard**

I f you have been astute enough to buy your own house when younger, and have paid off your mortgage, you will find that you can retire a lot earlier than you expect. You are probably living in a residence which was big enough for all your offspring, who now have places of their own. You are also thinking that it is important to down-size, and you may be tempted by offers of cheaper housing in other parts of the country.

'Other parts of the country' have advantages when you are moving. Firstly, the houses are cheaper, which means you get a lot more for your money, and secondly they are usually a long way from your family. This latter benefit allows you to complain bitterly when they don't have time to visit you, and cut them out of the will for the same reason. It also saves you the chore of visiting those relatives yourself, and the imposition of babysitting, while those same relatives go out to the raves or snuff parties favoured by anyone under the age of 50.

You will probably be tempted to buy a bungalow. They are all on one level, and ideal for when you get incapable, you reason. Not so. Bungalows are designed to kill the OP as quickly as possible. Without stairs to go up and down, you are never going to get any exercise, so that if you do have to scale these obstacles in other people's houses, you can puff and blow, as though you'd just reached the summit of Everest. Invariably, those bungalows come in at the same or higher prices than a house, and have a large garden, which, you say, you can amuse yourself with if you have nothing to do.

To stay young:

- Avoid bungalows.
- Avoid downscaling.
- Avoid having a toilet on the ground floor.
- Live in a house.

If you choose a house in a retirement area, you will have no problems, because the competition is all looking for bungalows. You will get your exercise in the many trips up and down stairs, as your failing memory prevents you remembering what you went up for in the first instance.

You will have to climb the stairs to go to the loo, to have a shower, to make the beds, to look out of the windows and be offended by the granddaughter of your neighbour sunbathing, to see the sky, to watch up and down the street, and to generally feel superior to those people living at ground level.

In the unlikely event your relatives do make the journey to see you, you have plenty of room to put them up, and space for them to make their own food without imposing on your routines.

"But," you argue, "What happens when I get too infirm to go upstairs?" The answer is simple. You won't get too infirm to go upstairs, because you will be getting the necessary exercise to enable you to keep going upstairs. Once you get too infirm, you will probably plummet to the ground floor and kill yourself as detailed earlier, which saves all that mucking about with the final tedious stage of life where they keep you in hospital for six months and then murder you to get the bed back.

If you are unfortunate enough to contract a debilitating condition, *then* you can think about moving. You will have the financial capital stored up in your property to enable you to pay for care, or holidays, or Polynesian nurses, until you die, a very happy OP.

Failing that, having sold your place and sent your clutter to a clearance charity, you may find yourself in a room in a nursing home. Much sport can be had here, flirting with the staff, taking part in community activities, pretending you are a teenager on Facebook, writing your memoirs and planning how to use up every last bit of your money before the ungrateful family come to claim it… but that is another story in itself.

Handymen and Local Suppliers

"There's no workman, whatsoever he be, that may both work well and hastily." **Geoffrey Chaucer**

It is always best to shop local, we are told, so because you have no internet, and cannot be bothered to read the local directory, you choose the first handyman anyone recommends to you. Tradespeople are very good at doing something along the lines of what you have asked, but then they might not give you an itemised bill, and prefer cash, serious quantities of which you have in your handbag/wallet in case you need it, or happen to get mugged. This way you can be sure of nearly always paying through the nose for any work carried out.

You may need a new gadget, say a vacuum-cleaner, because the old one has a 19th Century plug and the council have just rewired your place. Rather than going to a big store, where your offspring are offering to take you, you pop round the local shop, and buy something they have on the shelf. Well, it might cost more, but if anything goes wrong with it you can always take it back, can't you?

Building work

Most of the time, you can get away with this, because you are trusting, and like to think that your masons are similarly trustworthy. In the majority of cases, you meet an honest tradesperson, who will do an excellent job, and charge you a lot less than the professional companies. You have made a good contact, and can recommend these people to your friends. The word gets round, and your contact can make a very reasonable living in the local community.

Beware though, that there are a few rogue traders about (you have seen them on television). They have only one motivation, and that is to disencumber you of your pension and life savings. For this reason, when someone comes to your door, and tells you that your roof is dangerous, you must instantly agree to let them repair it and give them a large amount of cash in advance, for the essential materials they need to get started. If you see them again, and you probably will, because they can smell a mug (not the tea containing kind) a mile off, and will want to unburden you of more cash, they will proceed to remove most of your roof-tiles. They will then return apologetically, and say they need more money to continue, because they have discovered that the joists and rafters are rotten, as well as the bricks they are laid on having crumbled, owing to the shoddiness of the original builders. If you are lucky, they will not relieve themselves in your water header tank. Yes, you know you have seen people like this on telly, but that sort of thing only happens to other people of course, not you.

You have worked all your life, and amassed an adequate nest-egg to see you through your retirement, but the money is burning a hole in your pocket, so these handymen are a superb way of taking that load off your mind. At the end of the work, you might have a new watertight roof, and funny-tasting tea, but will probably suspect it is the same roof you had before, with the tiles just scrubbed up. Put this down to experience, and do not progress. The Law is unsympathetic to idiots, although you might get a quarter page news story in the local rag, where you can announce your foolishness to the entire world.

Appliances

Failing major building work, if any appliances in your home are needing replacement, and they really have to be seriously broken in order to get to this point, you can always find a local shop that will sell you their bottom-of-the-range machine and remove even more of your money, installing it for you and taking the original one away. They love old folks, because rather then get something up to date, you always try to get a machine that looks exactly like the one you are replacing. They have had this model in stock since 1950, and because it is now 'collectable', they can charge you even more for the privilege.

The Garden

There is always something to do in the garden. You have chosen a place with a big one, because you think you might need something to do during retirement. For the first 30 minutes, this seems like an excellent idea, but after those pesky thorn bushes, you put in to deter the neighbour's mastodon, become somewhat overgrown and grab at your dressing-gown every time you wander out to the composter, you decide that a handyman would be useful to clear some space.

He comes round once a week, unless it is raining or snowing or sunny or any other unusual weather, and potters about to your general instructions, digging up a bush here, or mowing a lawn there. At the end of two hours, you invite him in, and give him cake, and chat away about your various ailments, until his planned work period is over. You then give him money for the full time, and he goes away, promising to landscape the vegetable patch next visit, whether you wanted it or not.

Which Garage?

There is always something wrong with your car. Back in the old days, you could open the bonnet or hood, take out a spark-plug, or recharge the battery and all would be well. Today though, new cars are all sealed up like a Tesco's kipper, and if you even manage to refill your washer bottle, you are doing really well. The engines are now called 'power units' and inaccessible. So, what's all that about?

To find out and get any work done, you need to visit the local garage. People in there are nearly always male, and come in three main types:

1. **The Man you have known since he was a baby**: After a nice chat about the weather, and updating him on all your twinges, you leave the car with him to investigate that strange squeak. At the end of the day, the car is fixed and ready for you as promised, and you receive a reasonable bill for various spare parts, replaced to remove the problem.

2. **The Back-street Lockup**: He always has a shifty look and will be glancing over your shoulder as you talk, in case a constable should loom. He will take your car into the gloom of his oil-soaked workshop, with a promise to have it fixed on the cheap, within a week. You don't fancy being knifed, so you agree to these terms, promising to come back at the appointed hour. He gets your number and vows to call you, should there be any problems.

You hear nothing and are starting to wonder if you will ever see your trusty 'Pig-Ugly' again, but go to the lockup at the allotted time. To your amazement, the car is ready. The man quickly tells you what he has done, and then answers his mobile before you have a chance to ask any questions. Whilst talking, he passes you a reasonable invoice, with a single misspelled form of the word 'Repairs' scrawled on it. You give him cash and drive away very pleased with the cost.

You have no idea what he has done, but the problem you

had seems to have gone away, for a few days at least. You make a note to use him again, should you need to hide, following the bank heist you are planning.

3. **The Wise Mechanic**: Usually aged about 12, he listens to the problems with your car, and then tells you what is wrong, in unintelligible words and phrases, saying that these cars always have this problem, and it is usually a job for the main factory.

Fortunately however, he is qualified to work on this particular model, and you must leave the car with him and call him after lunch, to find out what work is needed, and the likely cost. If you are lucky, he will call you first and give you a long list of parts that need replacing, and the price of those, and will ask for your bank-card number before proceeding.

Appeals that you are living on a pension and cannot possibly afford that amount, are met by a total lack of sympathy. You say you will take the car away instead and find another garage. There is a sharp intake of breath, and he informs you that you cannot do that. The car is now not legal to drive on public roads. The only way to reclaim it is to agree to the set of new tyres, the various items of suspension and all other minimum requirements. You have to accept his word, and hand over your details. The car is ready when you arrive, but upon returning it to your driveway, you find that the petrol tank is nearly empty ('road tests') and you now cannot afford any more, until the year after next. This is nature's way of telling you that it is time to either give up driving, or stick with the local guy.

On Caring for Older People

"Most people say that as you get old, you have to give up things. I think you get old because you give up things."
Theodore F. Green

When you feel that you might be old yourself, you can make a special effort to find an OP who is, or pretends to be, physically worse off than you. These people do not have to be older than you are, and it is gratifying to visit people who are younger, but confined to their houses because of a permanent attachment to the television or delivered Chinese meals. For those people, it is easier for them to let you do all the work, rather than getting their offspring to assist instead, or doing it themselves via the Internet or otherwise.

With this other OP, you get a whole new set of ailments to discuss. They are confined to their rooms, so cannot make excuses to get away from you, and are therefore a captive audience to share everything with. They will normally be unable to get out of the house, so you can feel good going to the shops for them. If you choose your OP well, they may even give you the money for the goods; they should be happy to do this because you will usually undercharge them, having got three for the price of two and letting them have the spare item for free.

You may have to do some cleaning while you are talking, or make them a cup of tea. The Social Services love you for this, because they can turn up and sit back, while you do all the work, only checking your performance against a tick-list they have on a clipboard, or more increasingly on a small television-type device they carry in the massive bag they now need to contain it. You look interested as they try to show you what it does, including demonstrating amusing pictures of cats and children. They then attempt to illustrate that it can act as a sat-nav and location device, and a host of other things they call 'apps'. You have no idea why they should shorten the word 'applications', and your mind shuts down to refocus on the last piece of Battenberg on the plate in front of your now dozing OP, just before the Social Worker claims it ahead of you.

If you are particularly active, you can amass a collection

of worthy Ops, and never need to worry about time hanging heavily on your hands again. This will provide you with endless doom and gloom to share with your younger friends as they ring up, where you can tell them who has died this week, from a list of people they don't know and don't care about anyway. "The only OP we are interested in if they die is you," they point out, unkindly. You promise to let them know when you do plan to shuffle off, and make a mental note to revisit the solicitor regarding the Will.

On The Weather

"The weather is like the government, always in the wrong." **Jerome K. Jerome**

As an OP, the weather is never right for you. When it is sunny, it is too hot. The concept of removing one of your many overcoats, jumpers, corsets, or leather body-stockings never occurs. When it is cold, you sit in the house without the heating on, and shiver to death. When your descendants eventually read the Will, they are delighted to find you were roosting on a small fortune, and wonder why you froze to death in the first place. If you really need a scapegoat, you can fall back on blaming the Government for removing your heating allowance.

The weather is always the worst you have ever experienced, in all your born days. The river might have frozen for three months, and people were building houses on it, back when you were young, but it was never as cold as this. The skin might have been scorched off an entire regiment of the King's Own Wranglers, because of the heat in the summer of '40, but it was never ever as hot as this. You can stay indoors and let your YP do all the work.

Failing that, if you can get out, it is important to complain to everyone who will listen, or who happens to pass you in the street, about the extremes of weather you are suffering. You must ignore the fact that everyone else is suffering the very same weather. As an OP, you always feel the environment more acutely, usually because you are not moving about very much, or live in a bungalow, which has more exposed surface area than a house, and is always therefore colder/hotter than normal houses.

One of the best ruses is that when the weather changes, and this happens a lot in the UK, you can blame it for all your aches and pains. The advantage of which is that you can grumble about these at the same time as the weather. It doesn't get any better; a double complaint has more effect, and therefore gives greater satisfaction

Having been on the planet for a bit longer than most, you are supposed to be an expert on the climate. People will stop you (complaining) in the street, and ask you what to expect for the next 24 hours. You gaze around sagely at the sky, and tell them what you heard on one of the three forecasts this morning. If it was on the BBC or local radio, then most likely it will be completely wrong, but this does not matter, as your victim isn't listening anyway. You could confirm the details from the Met Office website, if you were able to use the Internet, but as for forecasts from the media, they seem to bear no relation to reality.

The only true way of guaranteeing what the weather is going to be like in the UK, is to use the word 'changeable'. A good plan is to go outside and actually stand in the weather for a moment or two. From your observations, you can put on the correct clothing for current conditions. If you don't go too far from your home, and this is very likely, given your operational range (or the state of the battery in your scooter), you can always return, and increase the number of coats later, if required.

On General Chumminess

"I think I'm being friendly with someone and I'll sit in their lap. They think I'm flirting with them." **Kylie Minogue**

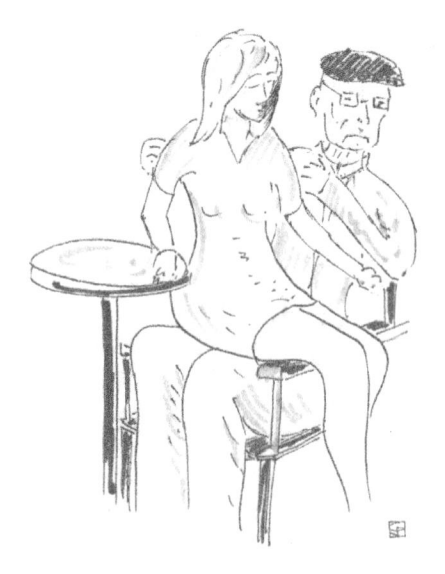

As an OP you have two modes for dealing with human interaction in the street:

The first way is simple; you can pretend to be wrapped up in your own thoughts and stare directly at the pavement in front of you. This will stop beggars accosting you for the price of a cup of tea, or people trying to sell you a sticker that will spoil the look of your faux-fur overcoat. An added benefit is that you can then keep precisely to your daily routine, without interruptions. Not making eye contact is important; if you smile, or stare at someone, then they are most likely to attack you like a wild dog.

The second way is more satisfying. Greet everyone you pass with a cheerful 'Good Morning' or 'Lovely Afternoon', never 'Good Evening', because you will already be tucked up in bed by then. If you are lucky, they might wish you a 'Good Whatever' back, and perhaps even stop for a chat about the weather. This is heaven sent, because you can tell them all the news, what you are doing today, and tomorrow if you can remember, or yesterday likewise. You can update them on all the intimate details of your family and other friends, and inform them who has died this week, all of which is vital for them to know.

In the shops, you will recognise all the assistants by name and occasionally get a little extra—maybe a cake that is approaching its sell-by date, or a free item of fruit. You think they are being kind, but it is really to move you along, so that they can serve the huge queue building up behind you. It does pay dividends eventually, because when you leave your purchases in the shop by accident, they will always look after them until your return. They may even put on a note 'Return to the woman/man who can't stop talking.' Everybody knows you, and shopping becomes a social event.

The downside is that you find you have to adjust your routines to compensate for extra time, so a careful balance has to be made between methods 1 and 2 above in order not to disrupt your timetable.

On Eating

Eating is great once you pass a certain age. There were a lot of things you used to hate, but had to eat them, because if you didn't, you'd get a clump on the head, and the same food put in front of you for the next meal. "There are starving children in Africa," you were told, "who would be delighted to see this." The stock reply, of course, was to suggest that the food was posted off to them, and this was particularly good at earning you a second clump on the head.

Later, if you had children of your own, you were not allowed to clump them on the head, because it contravened their human rights, and they could have you taken away to prison if you did. This meant that you had to use guile, bribery, or simply stuff them full of burgers and chips until they burst. If you practised the latter, you are probably the now the size of a supertanker yourself, and this gives you even more excuses to eat all the wrong things.

If you didn't manage to destroy your children's lives and health by giving in to their wiles, then you would have had similar arguments from them, as you tried to serve up anything without excess salt, sugar or fat. One of the tricks you did have to do, was to eat the same time and food as they did, and although you hated it, you had to set a good example.

Now that you have got rid of the offspring, you are free to eat anything you like. In order to get a balanced diet, you buy a few of the greens you think will agree with you, and then boil them for hours in the aluminium pans you've had since you were little, making sure to get as much of the aluminium into the water as possible. This can then be used to make the gravy, because it contains so much goodness. You ignore the lethal dose of chemical you have ingested, because the pans cost a lot of money in those days, and you want to get the value out of them. It is only when, either the vessels dissolve completely, soaking your ancient stove with carrot soup, or when concerned offspring exchange them for stainless-steel, and put the old pans in the recycling, without you noticing, that your health starts to improve.

This is where all those things you don't like suddenly start 'disagreeing' with you. There are many new and interesting foods on the market (or in the local shop at twice the price) but you have to avoid those. Mrs Gopher down the road had a bad time with one of those when she boiled it up with a cream-cake, you've heard, so it is best to avoid that. If anyone suggests that you try it, you bring out the 'disagree' card and wave it in their faces, making them feel that it was all a waste of time being born.

The exception with foodstuff is when you come across something you haven't had for years. This is normally because that something was so horrible, that it was only eaten when there was nothing else, like tripe, liver, scrag end or mutton chops. "You don't see these very often," you say. "I really used to like them." This is most probably owing to the clump on the head, a kind of Pavlov's Dog reaction, making you think you liked it. You take it home, have a brief taste and then leave it in the fridge while you think of another way to cook it. Nowadays of course, if one of the old things was horrible, they change its name, so when you eat swede, you forget that it is one of the turnip family, and think you are enjoying it.

When all else fails, you can bring out the 'Doctor' card. "My doctor told me to keep away from that," you can say. This is the end of that conversation, even though it might have been something completely different that the doctor was talking about. You can always get a pill for it anyway, and the amount the doctor has given you probably means you can't eat anything without some side-effect.

The Rules

- Don't try anything new.
- Make sure everything is thoroughly cooked.
- Eat all the things you like.
- Everything you like is good for you.
- Everything you don't like disagrees with you.
- Anything you don't like carries a warning from your doctor.
- Eat at exactly the same time each day, whether you are hungry or not.
- If you find a dangerous-looking root vegetable, keep it in the fridge until it dissolves.
- Use your old pans until they dissolve.
- Eat cakes.

On Death

"I don't want to achieve immortality through my work; I want to achieve immortality through not dying." **Woody Allen**

This is the sad bit about growing old. As you get older, the law of averages says that your contemporary friends and relations start dying off. On the up side this is quite useful, because it gives you lots of news to tell people. "Mrs Doolally died last week," you say. "Mind you, she was ninety-eight, an honorary member of the speed-camera installation crew, and had been on a mobility scooter for the last fifty years, most of them on roadworks on the A14."

Your victim shakes his/her head and says it is a shame, or gives you their condolences (whatever those are), not having a clue, or even caring, who you are talking about. The fact is that, rather than being upset about the passing, you should be grateful it was not you, because someday could well be.

The really sad thing is when someone is taken before their allotted years; that is when to mourn, so be glad that all your friends and relations are older; the chances of any of them dying young are drastically reduced; certainly something to celebrate. Give thanks for waking up each morning… unless the bailiffs are at the door, or you live in Siberia.

Don't dwell on thoughts of the 'Dingy Mower' (a paler version of the 'Grim Reaper'); if you need to cheer up, are particularly macabre, or simply like a good laugh, then you should consider leaving instructions as to how you would like to be interred, once you have no further use for your physical form, of course.

There are a number of options you can specify in your Will, or to a relative you can trust (as if… not Asif):

Cremation

It is best to have this done after you die. Cremation is hot work, and your mortal remains will be handed to the family in a small container. How they manage to reduce you to this state, when you were wearing your best suit complete with rings and pocket-watch, and that iPad someone gave you last birthday, and were in a large wooden coffin, is beyond comprehension. I suspect it is a trade-secret jealously guarded by undertakers, and probably involves the scrapings of the furnace.

Are those really your ashes in the box? There is no way of telling, when the production line is running all through the day, but your relatives know no better, so depart to follow your wishes with what they have been given.

If you fancy a bit of fun, specify that you want to be scattered on the top of a mountain, or in a forest miles from anywhere, or better still, abroad, so that you can quote Rupert Brooke about corners of foreign fields and all that. This will always inconvenience the relatives, and give them something else to hate you for. It may even provoke a family feud between those who say they should follow your requests, and those who just want to dump you in the normal rubbish bin, and collect the fortune.

Standard Burial

This normally involves a sturdy coffin, and a hole in the ground. Again you can specify some place a long way from where your family live. If you choose the right time of year to die, and a good location, you can ensure that the weather is so awful that the mourners suffer to the utmost, and come away with colds and pneumonia and are only too glad to see the back of you. This prevents them from rending their hair, or wailing in anguish at your departing. If they don't follow you soon afterwards from complications received, they might have time later to smile a bit when they remember the cleric stumbling over your name, and singing the same verse of the litany three times because he's drunk/confused/a stand-in/off the street or some other source.

Standing Up

This might be a novel way to specify in your will. It has the advantage of saving space in an already crowded cemetery, and keeps you away from being vaporised and polluting the atmosphere with unnecessary carbon dioxide (and alcohol, if you've spend your time correctly). It will give the family hours of amusement, as they try to persuade the authorities that it is a brilliant strategy. You can even threaten in your Will that you will return and haunt them, should they not carry out your wishes to the letter. You are doing your bit for the environment, and perhaps, one day, everyone will be interred like this, you argue.

A Vault

This is a great idea if you have pots of money and don't want to share it, or you are a fan of 'Buffy the Vampire Slayer'. You can have one of these constructed to last a death-time, and even make provisions for other members of the family to be interred with you (the dead ones, preferably). A vault does not even have to be in a cemetery, because, if you own loads of land, you can use some of that. Your lead coffin can be placed in the master niche, and you will be secure in the knowledge that you eventually may be reborn to drink the blood of virgins, or at least be in the company of other family members.

Green Burial

You might like to save the planet a bit more by specifying one of these. It does not (usually) involve family members taking you out into the forest at night and covering you with leaves, but rather burying your remains in a location where people are not allowed to put up stone and metal memorials to you. This is good because it stops low-life scrap-metal thieves from removing all the hardware, and selling it on to equally low-life scrap-metal yards.

Eventually the area will revert to green pastures, until someone decides to put a housing estate on top of it so time later. You can then rise from the grave and haunt their cramped utility rooms, while your remains go to be studied by eager young archaeologists, who will conclude you died of cake-related fallout. Honestly though, there is little chance of this, because the areas usually used for green cemeteries are land which is so waterlogged, there is more chance of you becoming the foundations for a marina rather than regular housing.

The Wake

Some beliefs say that the Wake should reflect your glory in life; the better the wake, the better the person. You can put some of your money aside, to pay for a lavish do for all the people who you hated. You can even specify the fare, and perhaps suggest amounts of exotic seafood, fugu fish, squid, prawns, and other items that do not keep all that well in warm weather.

This is another way to take people's minds off mourning for you. If your relatives are dropping like flies (used to do before we were stopped from using anything other than 'environmentally-friendly' fly-killer, which loves them to death) then the survivors become 'death-hardened', and get into the routine of a quick procession, departure and mourning, before they have to deal with the next one. This will happen a generation at a time, so expect batches of relations to be dealt with accordingly to make room for your descendants, or at least more foreign immigrants.

Pestilence

This is the quickest way to get buried. They get a digger and make a large hole, and you and all the other victims are dumped in, and quickly covered up. The advantage of this is that it costs nothing, you have a large space, plentiful company, and no maudlin relatives and friends left behind. Apart from being the end of all Humanity, this is a good option to consider.

Things to do to Not be Old

"Growing older is not upsetting; being perceived as old is." Kenny Rogers

By now, young or old, you will have dried your tears and need something to cheer you up after the last chapter. I repeat that age is not a number, but an attitude, and here are some points to improve that attitude, be you an enlightened OP, in danger of becoming an OP, someone

who cares about an OP, or you just want a giggle. In no particular order:

- If you have to drive, buy something interesting rather than functional. Think how much shopping or furniture from IKEA you can't get in a Mazda MX5 or on a BMW S1000. You will save the cost of the vehicle in a very short time, and not clutter your house up into the bargain.
- Avoid attacking people in the street; this suggests you are either old and demented or a psychopath, and will not get you into polite society with any certainty.
- Check out your routine. If you find you are doing the same thing at the same time every day, change it. Do something different, like erecting a severed head at your gate as a warning to wrongdoers.
- Dusting, vacuuming and ironing are a waste of effort, so don't feel tempted to do them; if you have visitors due, then perhaps make sure you can still see the front door, but you will find that most people never notice dust. If anyone does happen to complain about anything, you can put them to work doing it for you, and save all that effort.
- Do the washing only when it really needs to be done, or simply buy a new set of clothes from the charity shop, and take your old ones in at the same time. You can purchase those back later when they have been dry-cleaned and mended for you.
- Get the right credit card. This is like real cash, only you have benefits in money-off tokens etc. Credit cards are not the 'Psoriasis of Beelzebub' you think they are, and if you know what you are doing, and don't live outside your means, they can be quite

useful.

- Go on the internet. Get a younger relative to give you one of their old computers, and set it up for you with a browser, and something like WhatsApp, so that you can insult friends and relatives at a distance. Now don't freak out; you can already use your TV, and the gas oven, so you *will* be able to use the computer—the technology is exactly the same, only it's your brains that are cooked, not the food.

- Get a proper stool, and don't go clambering around fixing gutters by yourself; that's what a handyman is for. If you can't afford a handyman, get the Council in to repair it for you, and if they won't, then leave it. If dangerous, you can sell your story to the paper, and if not, then why bother in the first place?

- Do not grunt. Check yourself, make a note every time you do, and put a pound coin in the charity box as a forfeit. Add 1 point to your score in the quiz for each groan. When you finally get to it, if you have forgotten how many, simply add 10 points, and leave it at that.

- Bend from the knees. A good technique is to keep a valuable glass ornament in your top pocket. This way, if you bend over, it falls out and smashes on the quarry-tiles. The cost of replacement focuses the mind perfectly.

- Don't go on about your ailments. Nobody give a wet slap about them, apart from your relatives, who are probably waiting for you to die, and leave them your money. If someone asks "How are you," they are merely making conversation, not being 'interested'. If you really want to reply, the best answer is, "What's it got to do with you; you're not my doctor are you?"

- You might go to some sort of religious establishment. Do it as a pleasure, not a penance. You don't have to apologise to your God all the time. He knows you are a good sort, and He's not bothered; if He was, then He would strike you down with the ague every time you missed a service. However, if you *are* being struck down by the ague every week, then get back there straight away, and make your apologies.

- See if you can find some clothes that you didn't wear last century. Take a young person to the charity shop, and get them to choose things that actually look good on you. There are plenty of these, and quite often they will only be a few years out of date. Suits are in short supply though, because their previous owners have usually been buried in them. Failing that, get your YP to take you to a shop where you can buy new clothes at reasonable rates, and accept their choices. If you are ridiculed in the street afterwards, then your solicitor is always ready to update your Will.

- Kill your hairdresser if he/she makes you look like a 1970s tea-lady.

- Get some trainers for wearing in the house. These can have industrial strength inserts to keep the odour in check (or your money back) and can even be slip-on if you've forgotten how to tie laces, or can't reach. Don't buy the shoe size you wore 50 years ago, but get a pair that fit, and feel comfortable in woolly socks. You may have to pay a few pounds for these, but as it is your feet that are most likely to try to kill you (excluding the relatives), you need the best affordable.

- Have your 'specs' on a cord, so that you only wear them when you really need to. Often this will improve your eyesight and sense of depth, and when you are not wearing them, will teach you how to get around the house in a power-cut.
- Keep away from doctors and hospitals (and Labradors). If the chemist can't find you a remedy for whatever it is, put up with it, unless life-threatening.
- Make sure you have a good hobby which isn't gardening. Writing, painting, travelling, history, debauchery, witchcraft and photography are fine, but stay away from stalking, vigilantism, bank robbery and bingo, as these are likely to cause you upset.
- Do not move to a bungalow or flat. This is the best way to lose the use of your legs. You need stairs to exercise on, particularly if you are forgetful, and have to keep going up and down.
- Keep walking. Make a point of going as far as you can, and then do an extra 100 steps. If you live in a caravan, you can move it to a new lay-by or nature reserve every 12 days, and make sure that the distance to the shops is increased each time.
- Keep your mind exercised. Learn how to do cryptic crosswords, do complex equations on your fingers, send good vibes out to people who need it, develop a cure for cancer using only items found at the chemist, or invent an elixir of youth. Sell your story. Write scathing letters to the newspapers, asking why they highlight awful goings-on, but never do anything about them.
- Do not complain about the weather. Remember John Ruskin, who said, "Sunshine is delicious, rain is

refreshing, wind braces us up, snow is exhilarating; there is really no such thing as bad weather, only different kinds of good weather." He also said "Millais, you cad, you stole my wife," but this isn't really relevant (unless Millais stole your wife too).[2]

- Worrying does no good. Don't worry about things. If you can change them, do so; if you can't, then ignore them. Worrying about everything will alter nothing, except your state of health.
- Be aware. Don't go through life thinking about your next meal, or Mr Skunkworrier's adenoids, when there is an uneven pavement, or a pelican crossing, with a speeding car approaching. Keep your wits about you, and you can minimise the risks of an untimely accident, and never get to a situation where you become an OP.
- Blame everything else on Brexit.

---

[2] Picture of Effie Gray/Ruskin/Millais, looking enigmatic about being stolen by her portrait painter—but it did turn out for the best.

Conclusion

Getting older in the UK is good, because you:
- Don't have to work.
- Don't have to get up in the morning, except when you want.
- Can enjoy all your hobbies.
- Can go on nice holidays, by spending your pension/nest-egg.
- Can sell your house in an expensive part of the country, and buy something bigger and better in a low cost area.
- Can get away with more that you ever thought.
- Can say what you think.
- Can go wherever you want.
- Get free transport on the buses if over 66 (currently).
- Get free prescriptions in most places.
- Get a third off rail fares.
- Get discounts on most attractions.
- Get free entry into museums abroad (take your passport).
- Can spend time with your relatives, if you want to.
- Can keep up with friends who are far away.

- Can visit, and scrounge meals off said people.
- Can have a drop of the hard stuff for medicinal reasons, without having to worry about work the following day.
- Can go to work's reunions, and sympathise with people who are still at your old company.
- Can write angry letters to the local paper, and be published.
- Can spend time choosing what you buy, and then feel smug when you half your shopping bill.
- You only need to buy stuff for the moment. If you need more, you have time to pop back to the shops.
- Can peer over the top of your specs, like a university professor, or David Dickinson.
- Can tell your friends secrets, because they forget them instantly.
- Can wear a silly hat in all weathers, and as many coats as you like.

If you are over a certain age, you may already be thinking like an old person. You can't walk as far as you used to, so why bother trying? You can't work out how to use things like washing machines, tumble dryers or the internet, despite the efforts of your YP to show them to you, so you really don't want them in your house.

This sort of thing is all Nature's way of trying to hurry you to your grave. Back in the good old days, when the peasants used to work all daylight hours, until they dropped dead of the plague, and the toffs lorded it up over serving wenches, and died of piles or the pox, there was rarely an occasion when anyone would reach the menopause, let alone become an old person. They would never have looked old, because there was a thing called the Ozone Layer, that protected their skin against harmful rays, and usually an outbreak of pestilence or famine would see them off well before normal aging cut in. In consequence, they had to pop out as many children as possible in the times after dark, when others in their one room hovel couldn't see what they were up to.

One imagines a good number of fine looking (if a little grubby) humans going to their final rest and causing much dismay amongst the survivors. (The concept of 'Carousel' in 'Logan's Run'). They had 'faith' in those days though, so death was something that happened, along with life, and the seasons, and the neighbour's pig.

Nowadays, we usually don't have the luxury of a short and wearing life, and our body clocks are confused by the fact that, fortunately, most of us live beyond our forties. The body was not designed for this, so the brain tries to switch it off, by sending all sorts of messages to tell one to get on and die. This is what you are listening to when something new comes along. 'It'll see me out' was a phrase first discovered by the Greek Philosophers on the side of a bottle of Hemlock, and used to great effect by the same. Now it is applied to old pullovers and appliances, which out of spite, continue to keep working.

The mind refuses to understand pill dispensers, so that you are bound to take an overdose, some time. It fools you into thinking that the Three Legged Stool of Satan is a stable artefact to get you balancing. It upsets your inner ear, so that you topple over at every available opportunity, and it makes you argue with white-van drivers, and therefore risk death in that way. It disrupts your eyesight and hearing so that you step into the road without looking, and it fills your head with trivial nonsense, so that the smallest thing becomes a major worry.

On the other hand, the survival instinct blanks your thoughts, so that, long after you should have shuffled off your mortal, you remain in a state of blissful ignorance, and can spend all day looking through the same set of photos, without getting bored. This does help your visitors though because they can visit for an hour, and you still think they are relatives long passed over, and feel comfortable in the knowledge.

It is not really this depressing though; your mind is just like any other part of the body. Keep it going and exercised, and you will get the best mileage out of the mortal shell. You can detect when you are slipping into a rut, and use your mind to get you out. Tackle new things with enthusiasm. There is always a young person willing to explain technology and wizardry to you, there is always a coven of witches to join, or a new society bent on improving the minds of the people who paint the white lines on the road. Be wacky, be different from the norm, and if Norm needs talking out of being an OP, then spend the time to do it. The world is your lobster, so drop it into the boiling water and get your crackers out.

Quiz to test if You really are Old

Tick one answer on each line, or leave blank if it doesn't apply. There are no wrong answers, so, go for it! Sorry the writing is small. It's all part of the test. If you can't see it, you may already be an OP... or have lost your glasses.

Activity	A	B	C	D	E
What do you wear on your feet in the house?	Slippers	Trainers	Nothing	Wellies	New shoes
What do you wear on your feet outside?	Sandals & socks	Trainers	Nothing	Wellies	Rubber soled shoes
How do you pay for things?	Cash	Credit card/ iPhone	Beads	Don't buy things	Don't pay for things
How do you get in to the shops?	Taxi/Bus	Car	Walk	SUV	A gemmy
What sort of car would you buy?	Hynishota	Other	Camper	SUV	Anything I can steal
How fast do you drive? Choose nearest.	20mph	90mph	30mph	70mph	Fast as possible
How do you reach things?	Stool	Arms	With love	A stick	With a gemmy

What do you do when you bend over?	Grunt	Reach phone	Make love	Pick up money	Hide from the constabulary
How many times do you go to church a week?	2+	0	The world is my church	1	Only the roof
How many coats do you wear	2+	0	An Afghan	1	Stripy jumper
What is your coat made of?	Nice wool	Leather	Ferret, or something	Waxed cotton	Anything black
How many times do you fall over a day?	1	0	2+	Never get out of my SUV	As many as possible
Who/what is responsible for the state of the world?	Everyone	Brexit	Society	The Weather	The Law
How many times do you see the doctor a month?	5+	1	What's a doctor?	0	In hospital only
How many times do you get your hair done a month?	2-3	4-7	0	1	8+
How many times do you use the internet/mobile a week?	0	2000+	1	2-5	About 100
What do you live in?	Bungalow	Parent's house	Van	SUV	Community housing

Everyone's Guide to (not) being an Old Person

How long have you lived in the area?	15-30 years	1-15 years	12 weeks max	Forever	Up to 1 year
How do you get stuff fixed?	Local handyman	My dad	Karma	Do it myself	Nick replacements
What dog do you have?	Small yappy one	Staffy	Something floppy	Collie	Pit bull
What music do you like?	Classical	Rap/House/Pop	Prog	None	The music of the night
How do you deal with technology	Somebody else's problem	Use it all the time	Love it	What's technology?	Nick it
What do you think of the weather?	It's getting worse	Never go out in it	It's beautiful	It's always bad	Hate snow
How do you interact with the man in the street?	Discuss your aliments	Ignore or punch him	Give him flowers	Say "get orf my land!"	Nick his wallet
How do you deal with death?	Tell everyone	What's death?	Smoke more	Call the vet	Dump the murder weapon

Now don't peek overleaf before you have finished the answering all the questions.

Scoring

You should have selected up to one answer from each row. Award yourself the following:

If nothing in that row applied to you: **0 points**

Then for the columns, a tick in...

- Column A: **4 points**
- Column B: **1 point**
- Column C: **2 points**
- Column D: **3 points**
- Column E: Take away **2 points** per answer here, unless most of your answers are in column E, in which case award yourself **2 points** per answer instead.

Tot up the total of points. If you can't work out these instructions, add 10, and give it to a YP to work out for you.

If your score is less than 15 then enjoy your youth, keep away from toxic substances and get a pet rabbit.

If your score is less than 10, then add 70 for being totally confused.

How Old Are You Really?

By now you will have calculated a number of points.

If you guessed that each point equated to one year, then deduct 5 from your total.

If you skipped directly to the quiz without reading the book, then take 5 from your total, because you are too busy to read it, and therefore must have a full and rewarding life.

If you have answered honestly, you are now looking at the age you are perceived to be. You can do something about this if you want to, or can simply say that the quiz is a load of rubbish—if the latter, add ten years to your age, for taking it too seriously. The guide is written as light-hearted fun, but there are some things you can do to avoid acting too old too early, and you might have spotted a few of these on the way through.

Detailed interpretation of the results follows:

Take the column with the majority of your answers and read below. If you have an equal number of columns represented, then take the proportions and apply bits of each explanation to your result.

Column A

You are behaving like an old person, whatever your actual age. If you want to, you can go back through the guide and read up on as to how to avoid getting any older (see the chapter on 'Things not to do'), or you can just tell the author to stuff it, and carry on with your life. If you do tell the author to stuff it, deduct 10 years from your age score for being feisty enough to tell the author to stuff it.

The Result

You possibly smell slightly of cabbage, dogs, or at least musty clothing.

Column B

You are definitely behaving like a young person. You are doing all the right things to stay young, so bear this in mind, and keep a sharp vigil for any symptoms of getting old. Knowing what to look for will help you live to a ripe old age, or at least die young and happy.

The Result

You may smell of marijuana, cigarette smoke or babies.

Column C

You are probably a closet hippy. You will go to pop festivals, and wear flowery wellies, even though the majority of fellow sufferers are half your age. You may live in a caravan or a trailer-park, and love life to the fore.

The Result

You are generally a happy and sunny person but smell slightly of mud, goat and Patchouli oil.

Column D

You probably live on a farm, and spend your time complaining about the price of pork, as you drive your Range-Rover around at night looking for rustlers, thieves and bandits. You will almost certainly own a good number of shotguns, and are aware that murder is only a crime if you shoot the poacher in the back when he is running away, rather than in his chest, where you can claim self-defence.

The Result

You may smell slightly of cow or sheep dung.

Column E

You are a bit of a Jack-the-Lad, a slightly roguish, dodgy sort of dude, a bit of a geezer. You are not above relieving an old person of their savings, in exchange for a touch of shoddy work, and are always looking for the next deal. You have realised that you only get out of life what you put in to it, plus a bit extra if you can find a few mugs.

You are however quite likeable, and come over as trustworthy, in order to pursue your chosen profession. If you have made it to this age, and are still practicing, then the likelihood is that you will be giving it all up for a while soon, where you can try out the security in the open prison, detailed in the early chapters. An added benefit of this is that you can meet lots of old people there and may be able to scam them out of more cash.

The Result

You smell slightly of bull***t.

For further reading, please see 'The Secret of Endless Life', 'One Million Things to do with Spare Time' and 'Boredom, is it the Yawn it's cracked up to be?" by the same author, all due to be published in 2230.

About the Author

Robert Wingfield has been a wordsmith for most of his life, but only recently took early retirement to focus fully on his passion for the written word. His main occupation, these days, is studying starvation, as a poverty-stricken unrecognised genius.

He writes in a number of genres including Gothic, sci-fi, fantasy, children's, supernatural, travel and satirical, occasionally all together, and also reviews, formats and edits other works.

www.cantbearsd.co.uk

As part of an aspiration to gain recognition for the many excellent authors the publishing houses forgot, he runs the Inca Project, a free showcase for all that is best of Unconventional Unrecognised or Unsigned writing.

As Shakespeare never said:

"The meaning of life is to find your gift. The purpose of life is to give it away."

The Incas are occasionally looking for new authors, so give the site a look, and see if we can help you.

www.incaproject.co.uk

Printed in Great
Britain
by Amazon